Hot and Cold Connections
for Jewellers

Hot and Cold Connections for Jewellers

Tim McCreight

A & C Black

London

First published in Great Britain in 2008 by
A&C Black Publishers Limited
36 Soho Square
London W1D 3QY
www.acblack.com

ISBN: 978-0-7136-8758-3

Copyright 2006 Brynmorgen Press
Reprinted 2008, 2009

Drawings and layout by the author

Published in the USA by Brynmorgen Press
Brunswick, Maine USA

CIP Catalogue records for this book are
available from the British Library and
the U.S. Library of Congress.

This book is produced using paper that
is made from wood grown in managed,
sustainable forests. It is natural, renewable
and recyclable. The logging and
manufacturing processes conform to the
environmental regulations of the country of
origin.

Printed and bound in Hong Kong by
Elegance Printing and Bookbinding Ltd.

CONTENTS

History and Overview

HISTORY AND OVERVIEW

It is impossible to identify the earliest cold connection—but fun to try. A romantic might think of that moment when our simian ancestors fastened a sharp rock onto a stick to make a spear. That must have come early in the history of joining, as did the mechanics of attaching skins together to make garments and shelters. We don't need to go that far back, except to make two points—joining techniques are old, and they have been invented by people like you and me.

Each discipline and material has generated its own catalog of joining methods. Carpenters approach problems differently than tailors; engineers think differently than artists, and this translates to a colossal wealth of resources for us. This book (or any book for that matter) cannot hope to be a complete summary of the ways parts can be joined. Apart from the impossible size of such a work, it would be instantly out of date. As I write this paragraph, some inventive person is developing a new approach. Rather than an encyclopedia, this book will try to be a map of the territory. Armed with this, you can have a deeper understanding of your options and recognize opportunities for hybrid innovations.

I will focus here on small-scale metalwork like jewelry, vessels, and housewares. The information has been divided into three sections: hot, cold, and adhesive connections. Each of these has a rich history in metals, and each could generate a fascinating archaeological survey in its own right. For the moment, we'll confine ourselves to a few snapshots. In dynastic Egypt, at a time when Europe and the Americas had almost no recognizable culture, goldsmiths were assembling complex and delicate ornaments. It is useful to remember that they started their work by purifying the gold they would use, then converting the crude ingots to useable sheet and wire. This process gave the ancient smiths an intimate understanding of how to control fire and melting points, the two cardinal ingredients in soldering. They also discovered that powdered malachite, a green mineral used by Egyptians for eye shadow, facilitated melting. Today we use the same chemistry in our fluxes. The pharaoh's goldsmiths, along with the Greek and Etruscan craftsmen who followed them, created work of incomparable beauty, all of it dependent on precise control of heat.

Fast forward to medieval Europe, to a time when monks and adventurers traveled to faraway lands in search of converts and treasures. They returned with a huge range of objects, including antique ceramics and eggs the size of melons. These curiosities were taken to silversmiths to have them mounted for use (a pattern that continues to this day). Imagine the challenge of fitting a silver base and rim onto a rare ostrich egg or a thousand-year-old Chinese vase. Heat could not be used, so the clever smiths devised cold connections to attach the parts.

We tend to think of adhesives as a modern invention, and this is a reasonable assumption because so many of the glues we use were developed in the last fifty years. But down the street from the Egyptian goldsmith, there was a furniture maker using casein glues to secure joints in wooden objects that still exist—and still hold together—today. The Renaissance goldsmith and author Benvenuto Cellini, described adhesives used in his day. In the nineteenth century, production firms such as Gorham Silver closely guarded their recipes for the adhesive pitch they used to fill knife handles and pedestal vases.

Against this backdrop of a long and fascinating history, contemporary metalsmiths learn from the past, take inspiration from the genius of their predecessors, and continue to invent new ways to join parts together.

Part One
Cold Connections

INTRODUCTION TO COLD CONNECTIONS

Cold connections, also called mechanical connections, are so basic that they often go unnoticed. When you pick up an apple and hold it in the palm of your hand, you've made a cold connection. Change the apple to a gemstone, and replace your fingers with small rods of metal, and you've got a prong setting. Cold connections are universal and inevitable. Like water or bees, life as we know it could not occur without cold connections.

Reasons to use Cold Connections

The most obvious reason to use cold connections is because you can. Why pick up the apple with your fingers? Because it's a lot easier than doing it with your elbows. In the world of metalsmithing, there are more serious answers, including:

*joining heat sensi-
tive materials*

removability of parts

*preservation of
patina, temper, etc.*

Heat Sensitive Materials

Far and away the most common reason to use cold connections is because hot connections are not an option. Try soldering a shell onto a copper panel and you'll quickly see the problem. Mastery of cold connections allows metalsmiths to use nonmetal objects in their work. This includes shells and twigs and stones. It includes plastics and leather and paper. And fabric, electronic parts, glass beads, toys, currency… you get the idea. The already rich palette of metals is magnified many times over by having access to this range of materials.

Preservation of Metal Attributes

There are times when materials could be connected by soldering, but there are reasons to avoid it. Imagine a bronze element with a delicate leafy green patina to which you want to
attach a sterling finding. Bronze and sterling can be soldered
together, but in this instance, it would destroy the patina. Cold
connections to the res-
cue. Another example
involves the best way to
join a sterling fitting to a
hardened and tempered
knife blade. Again, the
metal can be soldered,
but in this example, the edge-holding ability of the steel will be
diminished. This is another place for a cold connection.

Removability of Parts

Most cold connections are easily reversible. You can unclasp
the apple and it will be unaffected. Some cold connections, like
bolts for example, are especially good for this, so it is no sur-
prise that they are used when we need a connection that can
be taken apart. In other cases
we might not anticipate that
the connection needs to come
apart, but we want to leave
the option open. An example
of this situation is a coin that is
mounted to be worn as jewelry.
The connection needs to be secure enough to insure that the
coin is not lost, but the piece
should be designed so it does
not reduce the numismatic value of the coin. Soldering, drilling,
or gluing a coin makes collectors go crazy.

Health and Safety

Another reason, more idiosyncratic I guess, but worth mention-
ing, is that cold connections avoid the use of fire and chemicals
like fluxes and pickles. For a jewelry professional this sounds
silly, but if you are working with children, or in a restricted environment, this is an excellent reason to head toward cold connections. And then there are people who just plain don't like
torches. Sure, therapy is an option, but so are cold connections.

TENSION

Tabs

Tabs are extensions of one piece that wrap around another piece and lock the two together. A familiar example shows up in paper dolls, in which small fingers extend out from the smocks and hats used to dress the dolls. The same wonderfully simple option exists for jewelers, and presents many variations.

Process for Making Tabs

1 Trace one element onto paper.

2 Think through the locations of tabs to insure that the parts cannot slide apart in any direction.

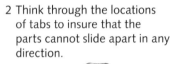

3 Transfer the design to metal and saw it out.

4 Anneal the metal if it is not already malleable.

5 File and sand the edges, solder parts such as bails or accents if they are needed, and create the intended finish

6 Bend the prongs to a vertical or "poised" position, insert the new piece, and press the tabs down with a bezel pusher, a bit of wood, etc.

ORNAMENTED

Maybe because of their association with paper dolls, we often think of tabs as small rectangles with a rounded end. Clearly there are more interesting shapes.

Internal Tabs

The idea is simple, and leads to a whole species of interesting possibilities.
1 Trace onto paper the interior opening of an element you want to join.

2 Sketch in tabs that will be made from the metal inside this line. Cut the paper pattern to test the effectiveness and appearance of the tabs.

3 Transfer the pattern to metal. Drill access holes to allow for inserting a sawblade, and cut out the tabs.

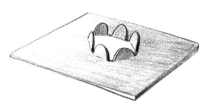

4 As before: file, sand, solder (if needed), patina, finish.

5 Bend each tab to a vertical position with pliers. Insert the piece and press the tabs over with a non-marring tool like a wooden dowel or a plastic brush handle. If the piece won't be damaged by impact, you can tap the tabs with a rawhide or plastic mallet.
Note: Several cold connected pieces can be layered together for an interesting

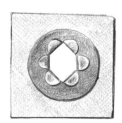

effect. For instance, two pieces joined with interior tabs could then be set using outside tabs, rivets, or other joining techniques,

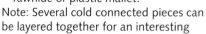

Lateral Tabs

These tabs are similar to the conventional "bent finger" idea described earlier, but in this case, the tabs are not bent over the object. Instead, metal fins are bent so that their bottom edges trap the pieces to be held.

1 As before, start by tracing the object that you want to hold.

2 Figure out where the tabs will be. In many cases, as in this example, the tab will first bend up vertically to make a wall that will hold the piece from sliding side to side. Layout the lateral tabs, typically by making a single saw cut (A). It is a good idea to test the idea on stiff paper.

3 Cut the metal to the proper shape, solder on additional parts (if necessary), and finish with patina, polish, etc. Bend the tabs upward, here to a 90° angle.

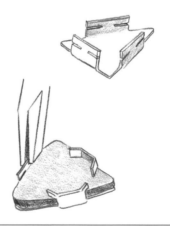

4 Set the object in place and bend the tabs sideways to lock the piece in position.

Variations: Lateral tabs can be quite minimal, very complicated, or almost anything in between.

Stilt Tabs

Here's a variation that can add drama and interest to a design by creating a space between layers, The shadow box effect is elegant, and the arrangement has the added benefit of accommodating a projecting element on the underside of a piece. Imagine, for example, that you want to set an antique button without cutting off the eyelet on the back side.

1 Start as before by tracing the piece to be set and determining the location of the tabs. Add "wings" to each tab equal to the height you want the piece to hover above the base. Bear in mind that a small space is often enough to make a powerful visual statement.

This will be the prong.
This will be the stilt.

2 Transfer the pattern to the metal, making sure to note the areas where saw cuts will allow the metal to be bent. Saw, file, sand, solder, patina, and finish as needed.

3 Use pliers to bend the wings upward. They might come all the way to a right angle, but this isn't necessary.

4 Pull the tabs upward. The bottom edge of the wings will be resting on the base sheet.

5 Set the element as before, by pressing the tabs down onto it.

Positioning the Tabs

Often the location of the tabs is symmetrical, but that's not a requirement, as long as the piece is protected from sliding out in any direction.

STAPLES

Is there anyone who isn't familiar with staples? They are thin pieces of steel wire bent into a broad "U," and lightly glued into a long trench that fits neatly into a tool that lives in the desk drawer. Well, yes and no. That's certainly what staples mean to most of us, but it's not the only form they can take. For our purposes, forget about the very specific device used to join sheets of paper together and think about how a staple works. Two or more pins go through a layer, or several layers, and are bent over to prevent their coming out. That definition offers a lot of room for design innovation.

Basic Staple

The most obvious things a metalsmith can do is to enlarge the staple, change the metal, and make the bar that connects the pins more interesting. For example, imagine bending a serpentine design in a sterling silver wire. To make the line more interesting, you could planish it on the apex of the curves. This changes the visual weight of the wire, making it swell as it rounds the loops. Bend the last quarter-inch of each end down and you have a staple, but one that is a lot more evolved than what you can buy at an office supply store.

• The legs can be bent toward each other or away, whichever shape works best for the design.

• If there is a trick to this cold connection, it is to insure that the tips of the pins lay flat against the back of the piece. Note that tapping slightly raised legs usually makes the situation worse, not better. Instead, start by curling the tips slightly (only slightly) in the direction that will be against the base when they are set. Bend them by working close to the place where the pin comes through the holes in the piece.

Blind Staple

This slightly more complicated version uses the same idea as a paper fastener, the brass disk with two thin legs that we all used in grade school. In our case, we'll solder wires onto the underside of an ornamental element. After polishing, the piece is attached the same way—drill holes in the parts to be joined, insert the legs, and bend. The pins can be close together (like the paper fastener) or separated, like a staple.

1 Make the ornamental piece, which I'll call the "cap." This can be sawn, cast, made in metal clay, or fabricated in dozens of ways. It could also be a bezel that will later hold a stone.

2 If there is work to be done on the base piece (there usually is), do this first. This would include things like soldering on pin findings, bails, or other attachments. The idea is to get these parts properly located first. Drill holes in the base piece where they will not be in the way of other parts of the piece, such as the pin finding.

3 Hold the cap against the base and scribe the location of the holes. If you use a pen, follow this by scratching marks with a needle or scribe so the location will show up during soldering, after the ink has burned away.

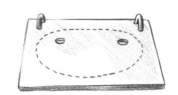

4 Solder lengths of wire precisely onto these marks. A neat way to hit the marks and simultaneously make the soldering simple, is to bend a length of wire into a large U-shape. Adjust the gap between the legs until it fits the marks. Fuse solder onto the tip of each leg, then hold the inverted "U" in position as you heat the cap with a torch. Some people like to use a weighted base with locking tweezers called a Third Hand to assist in this operation. After soldering, cut off the connecting portion (shaded).

5 Check the soldered joint to be sure it is solid. If there is a fillet at the base of the pin, file it away so the staple will rest securely against the base.

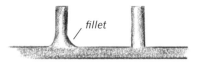

fillet

6 Finish all parts (patina, polish, etc.), then slide the parts together and bend the legs, first with a pliers, then by pressing each one down with a wooden dowel or plastic rod.

Multiple Legs

This variation is almost identical to the one above except that it uses more than two pins. The piece is more secure, especially if the cap has multiple extensions. The method is the same: solder U-shaped brackets of varying height to connect two pins with each solder operation. Cut only after all soldering has been done and checked.

Curled Ends

Instead of simply pressing the pins down, some designs will be enhanced by giving the pins an interesting shape. They can be wound into a spiral, for instance, and left standing at a right angle to the piece, or folded down flat. These can be on the back of the piece, but maybe they offer an embellishment that deserves to be on the front. The pins can be adorned with beads before being bent over.

Cotter Pins

This elemental version of a staple is familiar to machinists, but doesn't often find its way into jewelry. It is simplicity itself—a hybrid between a staple and a paper fastener. For the people who manufacture them, the beauty of the idea is that the loop in the wire is all that is needed to keep the pin from pushing through from the front.

For jewelers, this loop makes a great place to attach dangles, hang beads, or connect to a necklace cord. The loop can be hammered, textured, or simply left alone.

BEZELS

A bezel is a rim of metal that surrounds a gemstone and is pressed down over its curving edges to clasp the stone to a metal object. In most jewelry books, bezels show up in the stonesetting section (as they should), so they can be overlooked as a breed of cold connection. They shouldn't be.

Variations on bezels are so numerous that it is impractical to attempt to cover them all here. Readers are directed to books on stonesetting, where dozens of variations will be explained. On the following pages, I'll describe a couple basic approaches to illustrate the way bezels can be used on materials other than gems.

Basic Bezel

The parameters are general, but important.
- A bezel must make a neat and snug fit around the object being set.
- It must be securely attached all the way around the base.
- It should not extend over the piece more than is necessary. This will be determined by the angle of the piece—the straighter the sides, the more bezel is needed to achieve a secure grip.

Bezel-set button

good

too much bezel

Making a Simple Bezel from Copper Wire

1 Straighten a piece of wire by gripping one end in a vise with the other in pliers and pulling it taut.

2 Planish the wire with a polished hammer. If the wire curves, it is because the hammer blows are not landing squarely. Adjust as needed. Snip and file one end of the wire to make a square end.

3 Bend the loop to fit the object, either by eye or by bending it around the piece itself. The wire will always spring back, so go past the joint to allow for this. Check against the object periodically as you work to make a perfect fit. Fussiness at this point will make a better looking bezel and an easier setting job later.

4 When the fit is assured, snip the end and solder the loop closed. Use only a tiny piece of solder—first, because we don't want a silver blob on the copper bezel, and second, because solder is stiffer than copper and a bulge of solder will be difficult to press down during setting.

5 Check the fit by pressing the bezel onto the object. In the process, be careful that you don't distort the wall. It must remain vertical. Rub the bezel on sandpaper so the bottom edge is flat.

6 Clean a piece of metal that will be the base, and apply a layer of flux. Lay this on a bed of pumice pebbles rather than setting it flat onto a soldering block. This will allow heat to surround the sheet and let it heat up faster. Set the bezel into position and slide it back and forth to transfer a film of flux onto the walls of the bezel.

7 Set small pieces of solder against the bezel so they are in contact with both the wall and the base. If you plan to cut away the metal around the bezel, put the solder on the outside of the loop. If not, put the pieces on the inside.

solder chips

8 It is best to have the solder flow all the way around the base of the bezel in one flash. To accomplish this, direct the torch flame entirely at the sheet, angling the flame so you shoot it under the sheet. Allow the heat to travel from the underside of the sheet upward to the bezel.

9 When the solder flows, immediately pull the flame away. Allow the piece to cool for a few seconds, then quench it in water. Examine the joint, and if it is complete, put the piece in pickle to remove flux residue and oxides.

Pickle

SETTING WORK IN A BEZEL

Bezels used in this context are no different from when they are used to hold stones, so this information will duplicate what is available elsewhere in stonesetting descriptions. It is included here as a convenience.

Determining the Height of a Bezel

Metal has an ability to compress, which is what allows it to be hammered into teapots and corrugated into relief. When a bezel is pushed over, we make use of this ability. To understand how important this is, compare it with a material that does not have this ability, such as the paper this page is printed on. If you hold up a piece of paper and press against it, it will bend in the direction you press, and flare out in other directions to compensate. Press those flared areas in, and the paper will flare out somewhere else. The material needs to occupy a given amount of space, period. What makes a bezel possible is that the metal in the vertical wall can be squeezed together enough that the wall can be angled in against the object being set. But there is a catch. Metal has a limit to how much it can compress without being annealed. Annealing, a process that involves high heat, is out of the question once the element is in place, so we must work within the limitations of the metal.

Fortunately, this is easy to do. The best way to avoid a problem is to limit the height of the bezel. The taller it is, the more compression will be needed at the upper rim of the bezel. This can make the setting difficult and the edge irregular and lumpy. More than that, the reason the bezel is there is to display the thing you are setting. It only makes sense to show off as much of it as possible.

To determine the proper height, do not push the piece into the bezel. Read that again: Do not push the piece into the bezel. It's likely to get stuck there, and a lot of foul language and fussing will be required to get it out. Instead, set the piece beside the bezel, and gauge the proper height by eye. Make a mark with a scribe or pen, then trim the excess away with a file or manicure scissors. Follow this with sandpaper; before setting, the top edge should be uniform and smooth.

Setting the Bezel

When the height is correct, all soldering has been completed, and the finish is complete, press the object into the bezel. It's not uncommon that normal handling has caused the bezel to lean inward. Use a blunt tool to gently pull the wall outward to its proper vertical position.

The compression described above needs to be distributed evenly throughout the bezel. The way to NOT do this is to start at one point and press the bezel down as you go around the form. Rather than compressing, this will simply push the metal ahead of itself and create a bulge when you get back to where you started. Instead, press the bezel down in one place, then go across the form and press from there. Move to a spot midway between those two and press, then go across from that and press again. You can think of this as being the four points of a compass.

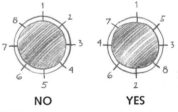

NO   YES

At this point the object should be gripped in place, though the bezel looks rather unattractive. Continue the process, starting midway between two cinches, and again jumping across the form for the next push. As the process continues, the waves of the bezel get progressively smaller until they are completely smoothed away.

A Little is a Lot

You'd be surprised how little metal is needed to secure an element in a bezel. Remember that this overlap is happening all the way around the piece.

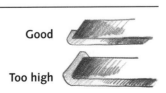

Good

Too high

Finishing a Bezel

There are many ways to make a bezel smooth and uniform, and they all work. Try everything you can think of to see which method works best for you. It is common to use several approaches in combination.

• Burnishing

In this technique, you rub a polished steel rod firmly around the bezel. If the form was even to start with, the burnisher makes it smooth, shiny, and tough. But if the form was irregular, a burnisher can accentuate the irregularities.

• Filing

Use a fine file (4/0 or finer) to shape the bezel, taking great care that you don't touch the object. Some people cover the object with masking tape, and while this doesn't hurt, it's worth observing that a file can cut through tape pretty quickly.

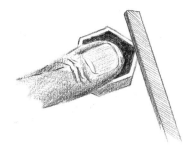

• Pumice wheel

This is a finishing tool used with a flexible shaft machine that consists of pumice granules embedded in rubber. Pumice is safe against most stones, but if you are setting wood, plastic, or shell, I recommend testing a scrap first.

VARIATIONS ON BEZELS

Use various metals.

You don't have to use fine silver.

Ornamented Bezels

Roll printed, stamped, engraved, etc. You might need to make an interior rim to support the piece being set.

Thick Walled Bezels

Start with metal at least 16 gauge thick; set with a hammer and punch.

Partial Bezel

Either make a full bezel and cut portions away, or build separate walls for the different sides of the piece being set.

SETTING WITH A FRICTION COLLAR

This method is similar to a bezel in some ways, but doesn't involve pushing the metal rim onto the piece being set. It is often seen when setting from behind, as illustrated here, but it is not limited to this use. It is especially good for objects with straight sides and for delicate objects.

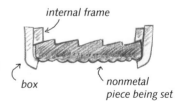

internal frame

box

nonmetal piece being set

1 Make a box that perfectly matches the work being set. Assemble this in whatever way is most appropriate to the design. This could be a strip bent into a loop like a conventional bezel, or a box with angular corners, or a casting, or a piece made in metal clay. In some cases, you can trim or grind the object to make it fit, but in others, all the precision comes in the metalworking. It is important that the fit be precise. The piece should drop in without being forced, but it should not rattle around once it is in the box.

2 (Option) Cut away the window portion of the floor of the box. This might be most of the floor in some cases, or a patterned grille in others.

3 If the work has an irregular thickness, trim the height of the wall to match it. Put the object into position and drag a marker around the inside of the wall to draw a line. Remove the object and cut above the line with a saw or snips. File smooth.

4 Make a frame that fits snugly inside the wall from round or square wire. This is usually the same metal as the piece, but it doesn't need to be. If you don't want the back of the piece to show, this could be a solid panel, either of metal or cut from another interesting material.

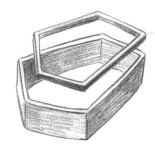

5 Complete all soldering, ornamentation, patinas, and finishing on all parts.

6 Slide the object into the box, then set the frame (or panel) onto it. Press down hard enough to be certain that the parts are completely seated.

7 Lock the frame piece into place, either by bending a bit of the rim over it, or by cutting stitches along the interior wall of the box. Stitches are small burs of metal cut with a graver, a sort of miniature chisel. Press the tip of the graver into the wall about a millimeter above the frame and slide it forward.

    A small finger of metal will curl up in front of the tool, and will become a prong that will anchor the frame. Each stitch is tiny, but when you have a dozen or more distributed around the interior, and assuming that all the parts are a tight fit, they make a secure joint.

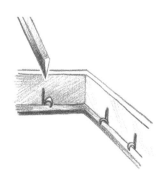

Variations

Secure the frame with rivets or screws.

 Push in here →

File a bevel on the inside of the frame, then bend the outer frame over it.

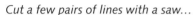

Cut a few pairs of lines with a saw...

then bend the resulting tabs inward.

PEDESTAL SETTINGS

One other device from the traditional stonesetting catalog deserves inclusion here because it lends itself so well to the irregular shapes that are associated with cold connections. The beauty of this setting (aside from its, you know, beauty), is that it is infinitely adaptable. It works equally well on a large scale or small, in precious metals or base metals, for thick objects and for thin ones. It is great for symmetrical objects, but really shows its stuff when you're setting an irregular shape.

1 Make a rim or pedestal whose outside dimensions exactly trace the object. When you view the piece from above, you will not be able to see the pedestal at all, but if you tilt your head in any direction, the sides of the pedestal show up. Achieve this by paying careful attention to the outline of the piece and with meticulous bending. In the case of an irregular piece that has thick and thin sections, it might be helpful to trace the silhouette onto paper. This way you can first get the outside perimeter exact, then, in a separate step, deal with the uneven thickness. The thickness and width of the strip used for the pedestal will depend on the object you are setting and the eventual use of the piece. In most cases, I recommend against making it thinner than 22 gauge because it is the pedestal that provides the strength of the setting.

Good. Edges are flush.

Bad. Base is too big.

Bad. Base is too small.

2 Determine the location of the tabs that will secure the object. Mentally try to slide the object in each direction; up, down, left, and right, to be sure that it will be securely locked in place. These tabs are an important element of the design, so give attention to size, shape, proportion, repetition, and so on to be sure that they are not only fulfilling their physical function (holding the object), but also contributing to the composition.

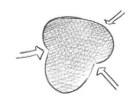

3 Create the tabs, probably by sawing pieces from sheet metal or by cutting lengths of wire. Bear in mind, though, that the tabs can also be forged, ornamented, cast, fused, or made from metal clay.

4 Solder the tabs onto the rim in the way that works best for you:

• Press the tabs into the soldering block to hold them in position, then apply flux and solder, and heat until the solder flows.

• Pre-melt solder onto each piece; this is also called sweating. One by one, hold the tabs in place with tweezers as you solder the parts together.

• Glue the parts together to secure their placement, then mix a small quantity of soldering investment and dab it onto the assembly. Allow to dry, then apply flux and solder and heat until the solder flows. Remove by dropping the hot piece into water.

5 Check the joints, refine the edges and surface, patina, and finish.

6 Set the object in place and press the tabs lightly onto the object, working from one location to the one diagonally opposite. When you're sure the piece is nicely seated, press each tab down firmly onto the object.

THREADED CONNECTIONS

The idea of a screw thread is traditionally assigned to Archimedes, a Greek mathematician. The relatively simple idea of a spiral confined along a cylindrical axis has had significant impact on our world, making possible everything from rocket ships to roller skates.

Commercial Nuts and Bolts

Nomenclature

Screws and bolts are usually described by the diameter of the central rod and the pitch of the threads. In the United States, the two most common systems are the National Fine (NF) and the National Coarse (NC). In both these systems, the size is given by two numbers separated by a

hyphen. The first number refers to the diameter of the rod (except for small screws) and the second is the threads per inch. For small screws, the diameter of the rod is identified with a number that (unfortunately) does not have any reference to its measurable size. These run from 0 (the smallest) to 10 (the largest number) before switching to inch fractions. See the charts on the following pages.

Using Commercial Nuts and Bolts

The most obvious way to use bolts is to simply insert the rod through the parts to be joined, then screw on a nut. Here are a few variations on the simple idea:

- Use two nuts to lock the joint. Turn the first nut along the rod until it is where you want it, then screw a second nut until it rests firmly against the first one. The result is that both nuts are locked in place.
- If you don't want the head of the bolt to show, solder the bolt onto the back side of a piece. If the head of the bolt will be in the way, cut it off and solder the remaining threaded rod onto the piece.
- Most bolt heads are hexagonal, a shape that allows for easy gripping with a wrench. When this shape is not consistent with the design, file the bolt head into another shape.

SCREW AND TAP SIZES – INCH MEASUREMENTS

National Coarse

Tap	Drill
0–80	3/64"
1–64	#53
2–56	#51
3–48	5/64"
4–40	#43
5–40	#39
6–32	#36
8–32	#29
10–24	#25
12–24	#17
1/4–20	#7
5/16–18	F
3/8–16	5/16"
7/16–14	U
1/2–13	27/64"
9/16–12	31/64"
5/8–11	17/32"
3/4–10	21/32"
7/8–9	49/64"
1"–8	7/8"

National Fine

Tap	Drill
1–72	#53
2–64	#50
3–56	#46
4–48	#42
5–44	#37
6–40	#33
8–36	#29
10–32	#21
12–28	#15
1/4–28	#3
5/16–24	I
3/8–24	Q
7/16–20	W
1/2–20	29/64"
9/16–18	33/64"
5/8–18	37/64"
3/4–16	11/16"
7/8–14	13/16"
1"–8	15/16"

SCREW AND TAP SIZES – METRIC MEASUREMENTS

Metric Coarse

Tap	Drill
1 x 0.25mm	0.75mm
1.1 x 0.25	0.85
1.2 x 0.25	0.95
1.4 x 0.3	1.1
1.6 x 0.35	1.25
1.7 x 0.35	1.3
1.8 x 0.35	1.45
2 x 0.4	1.6
2.2 x 0.45	1.75
2.5 x 0.45	2.05
3 x 0.5	2.5
3.5 x 0.6	2.9
4 x 0.7	3.3
4.5 x 0.75	3.7
5 x 0.8	4.2
6 x 1	5
7 x 1	6
8 x 1.25	6.8
9 x 1.25	7.8
10 x 1.5	8.5
11 x 1.5	9.5
12 x 1.75	10.2

Metric Fine

Tap	Drill
4 x 0.35mm	3.6mm
4 x 0.5	3.5
5 x 0.5	4.5
6 x 0.5	5.5
6 x 0.75	5.25
7 x 0.75	6.25
8 x 0.5	7
8 x 0.75	7.25
8 x 1	7.5
9 x 1	8
10 x 0.75	9.25
10 x 1	9
10 x 1.25	8.8
11 x 1	10
12 x 0.75	11.25
12 x 1	11
14 x 1.25	12.8
14 x 1.5	12.5
16 x 1.5	14.5
18 x 1	17
18 x 2	16
20 x 1.5	18.5

Locking Washers

In threaded joints, it is possible for wear and vibrations to wiggle a nut loose. Wear that screwed-together brooch while you're dancing, and the parts might come undone. The solution is to put some pressure on the nut so it is less able to rotate accidentally. A typical locking washer is nothing more than a traditional washer that has been cut and bent out of a single plane. When the parts are screwed together, the twisted washer is compressed. It tries to return to its original shape, which is to say that there is pressure on the nut. This pressure locks the nut from casual turning.

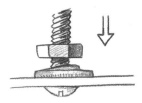

A similar arrangement can be created with leather or rubber, both of which can be compressed by tightly screwing the nut down. After tightening, the washer expands, and again puts pressure on the nut.

USING A TAP AND DIE

To cut threads, you will need tools called taps and dies. These are sold at hardware stores and jewelry supply companies, either singly or in sets. Both will require a specific handle or wrench, and while you can improvise if you need to, it's probably best to buy the appropriate tool. Assuming you will be making both the nut and the bolt (the positive and the negative), you'll need two separate tools that have the same size and pitch.

Cutting External Threads

A threading die is a hard but brittle cutting tool, designed to cut away small portions of metal. It is important that you start with a rod that is very close to the eventual outside diameter of the threads, either by buying the proper rod or by filing it to the proper dimension. If there is too much metal to start with, not only will the process be slow, but the die is likely to break. To determine the proper starting diameter, either consult the chart here, or use the shaft of the tap as a guide. The starting rod should have the same diameter as the bottom, unthreaded, section of the tap.

1 Select a rod of the proper diameter and file a shallow taper on the end.

2 Secure the rod in a vise, preferably either straight up or straight out. If this is aligned with the jaws of the vise (as opposed to angling off randomly), it is easier to keep the die straight.

3 With the die in a handle, screw it onto the tip of the rod until it engages. Screw one full turn, making sure the die is level. Unscrew a half turn.

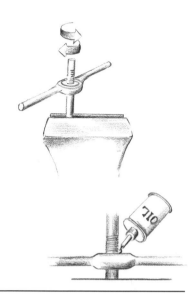

4 Screw a full turn ahead, which means only the last half of the turn is cutting. Unscrew to allow the chips to fall away and screw forward, only cutting for about half a rotation. Continue this full turn forward/half turn back pattern until the threads are as long as you need. It's helpful to add a drop of light oil every couple of turns to lubricate the process.

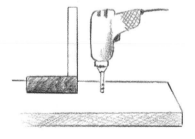

Cutting Internal Threads

This process is very similar to cutting threads on a rod. Prepare the metal, use a forward-and-reverse motion, and take your time. Again, the tool, called a tap, is a hard but very brittle steel part that is designed only to cut away small bits of metal. It is very important that you start with a hole the right size. Some taps have the recommended drill size stamped on the shaft of the tool, and many kits have a chart attached to the box. The same charts are given here on page 19 and 20.

1 Drill a hole of the proper diameter, squarely through the metal. A drill press is best for this, because it maintains the bit at 90°. If you are using a hand drill, set a vertical line behind the work and use it as a point of reference. This could be a try square, a plumb line, or even a book.

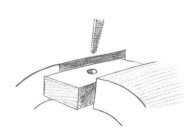

2 Secure the piece in a vise, unless it's large enough to stand on its own. If possible, line it up symmetrically in the vise so you can use the edges of the vise for visual reference.

3 Screw the tap into the hole until it just engages, then go a half turn forward. Reverse the motion to clear the threads. Place a drop of light oil onto the tap and screw it in another half turn forward. Reverse, then go forward, always stopping as soon as you feel a drag on the tool. If the chips do not fall away by themselves, unscrew the tap periodically and wipe the waste off on a rag. Continue until the tap moves easily, which indicates that it is no longer cutting.

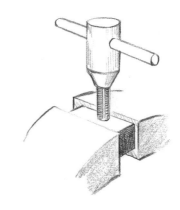

Making Threaded Parts by Casting

If you need a 14k gold bolt (hey, it could happen), one solution is to attach a sprue to a plastic bolt, invest it as usual, then go through the process of burnout, casting, and cleanup just as you would for any other casting. It is more likely, though, that if you are casting elements that will be joined by threaded connections, that you want the threads to be integrated into the design.

1 Apply a thin layer of oil on a steel or brass bolt. This can be any light oil, including 3-in-1, WD40, mineral oil, olive oil, or motor oil.

2 Warm the bolt in a lamp or torch flame until it is just barely too hot to hold. Insert the heated bolt into a block of wax, holding it as straight as possible. To allow the wax to harden onto the bolt smoothly, the parts must be stable. Rig up a Third Hand or similar arrangement so you can set the parts aside, untouched, until the wax hardens.

3 Leave it for at least ten minutes, then gently unscrew the bolt. Examine the interior threads you've made in the wax to be sure they are clean and intact. If not, repeat the process with a fresh block of wax; it's better to make it right than to invest time in carving and casting a piece that you know is faulty.

4 Dribble a few drops of oil into the threaded hole to deposit a thin lubricating film on the threads you've just made. Shake off any excess oil.

5 Build up a cup with tape around the opening of the threaded hole. This funnel makes it easier to pour melted wax into the hole but, and equally important, the lump of wax here will be a handle that will make it possible to unscrew the rod you are creating. Melt a rigid wax in a can or a spoon, and pour it into the threaded hole.

6 Wait at least ten minutes, then gently unscrew the threaded rod. You can now carve these wax elements as needed.

7 Spruing, investing, and casting proceed as for any other casting, with these commonsense concerns:
   • Do not attach a sprue to the threads.
   • In order to guarantee that no air bubbles form on the threads, mix a small batch of thick investment and paint it onto both threaded portions. Flow the investment gingerly off the brush, troweling it on to avoid trapping bubbles.

Making Threaded Parts with Metal Clay

This process is similar to casting, except that it allows you to skip the spruing, investing, and burnout steps. Metal clay is only available in silver and gold, so brass and bronze threads are not an option here.

Making Internal Threads

1 Lightly oil the threads of a bolt. Press PMC around a shaft, making sure that it has complete coverage.

2 Allow to dry completely.

3 Unscrew the bolt gently.

Making External Threads

1 Make a thread cutting die from a standard steel or brass nut. Remember that the resulting threaded rod will be a little smaller than the nut because of the shrinkage of PMC.

2 File three V-shaped notches on the interior of the nut. These will expose edges that will cut the threads.

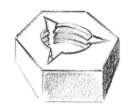

3 Make a rod of PMC+ or PMC3, slightly larger in diameter than the hole in the nut. Roll it so one end tapers slightly. This will make it easier to start the cutting process. Allow this to dry completely.

4 Screw the nut gently onto the PMC rod until it engages and starts to cut. Unscrew to clear the material, then turn the nut another full rotation. Continue this screw-unscrew action until you have cut all the threads you want. Work over a piece of paper so you can retrieve the dry PMC scraps. These can be rehydrated and reused.

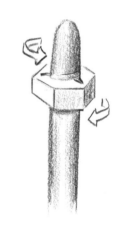

RIVETS
The Concept

Rivets comprise a huge family of connections that can join pieces without heat. They can be large or small, precious or nonprecious, basic or elaborate. In all these cases, the concept is the same. A length of material, most often a round wire, penetrates the layers to be joined and is then enlarged on both ends to cinch the layers together. Wherever you are reading this book, there is a rivet within a few feet of you. Rivets are used in cutlery, clothing, toys, housewares, eyeglasses, luggage, architecture, and automobiles.

Process Overview

Though there are many styles of rivets, the sequence of steps is surprisingly universal. Perhaps this is part of what makes them so appealing—once you get the general idea, it's quite easy to adapt what you know to other kinds of rivets.

- Make a hole that is a tight fit for the rivet, or make a rivet that is a tight fit with the hole.

- Anneal the rivet material.

- Slide the rivet rod into the hole so it locks into position.

- Trim the length so a small amount projects outward from each side of the layered assembly. File the ends flat.

- Set the rivet on a solid surface, making sure that it projects equally out of both sides of the assembly.

- Tap one end lightly so the metal curls over on itself.

- Flip the work over and repeat this process on the other end of the rivet.

- Continue tapping alternately on both ends until the rivet head sits on the surface and the parts are securely joined.

Drilling Sequence

It is important that the holes are in exactly the right location. Read that again—it's crucial that the holes are in the right place. It's tempting to clamp the parts together then drill holes for rivets through the stack. Bad idea. Despite your best efforts, somewhere in this process the parts will shift. Worse, this is so slight that you won't be aware of it, at least until you try to line up the second or third rivet and find that the holes don't match up. You can save yourself this frustrating situation by following this sequence.

1 Drill all the holes in one piece. In many objects, the location of the rivets is important to the design on one side (e.g., the front of a brooch), and less important on the back. To insure that the rivets fall where you want them, drill the holes in the front piece.

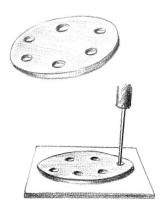

2 Set the pieces together and mark the location of one hole, by scratching with a scribe or needle. Separate the pieces, centerpunch, and drill that hole.

3 Create a rivet in that pair of holes. Note that at this point the parts cannot slide left or right, they cannot shift up and down, but they can still pivot. For this reason, it is still unwise to drill more than one hole.

4 Align the parts, and drill a second hole. Set a rivet in this hole—now the components are fixed. They cannot shift or swing, so it is safe to drill the rest of the holes and proceed with the remaining rivets in any order you choose.

UPSETTING

The trick in forming a rivet head is to provide the metal with no other option than to swell out into a rivet head. When metal is forced back on itself, it will bend wherever it can to absorb the force. We've all seen this when we're driving a nail that hits a hard spot. Given the chance, the nail will bend. In the case of rivets, the challenge becomes this: How can I prevent the rivet wire from bending sideways. If it can't bend, it has no alternative other than to compress, or fold back into itself in a process called upsetting. This is exactly what we want.

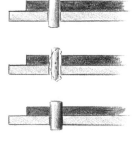

Two factors control the ability of a rivet to bend: having too much length above the metal, and having a hole that is too loose. I can't stress enough the importance of a tight fit between the hole and the rivet pin. If the wire has the opportunity to bend, it will take that route, which is the path of least resistance. The only way to force the pin to swell into a rivet head is to insure that there is nothing else it can do. A clear understanding of this fact will provide guidance on the holes and on the length of metal projecting out from the parts.

Hammers and Hammering

Almost any hammer can be used to make a rivet, but if you're going to be using rivets often, it makes sense to invest in the proper tool. First, the hammer should be in appropriate scale to the size of your work. Blacksmiths might use a two-pound hammer to make rivets for a large construction, while jewelers will typically use a hammer head that is about the size of your little finger. The ability to hit the rivet wire accurately is more important than applying a lot of force, so the trick is to use a hammer you can control.

Cross-peen Hammers

The mechanics of a cross-peen are well understood, and used by metalsmiths when forging and silversmithing to control the direction of movement. The force of a blow is directed in only two directions: straight outward from the two faces of the peen. This allows us to steer the flow of the metal with each blow.

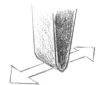

For rivets, we use the cross-peen to force metal outward. Aim for the center of the rod, and deliver a series of light blows.

You will see the round wire assume an oval shape. Pretty cool, huh? Rotate the piece 90° and repeat the process. The oval will now grow in the opposite direction, forming a round dot again. You might think of this as hammering a plus sign (+) on the end of the rod. When the rivet head is large enough to insure that the parts are locked together, turn the hammer over and use the flat peen to smooth away the hammer marks of the cross peen.

Ball-peen Hammers

Some people prefer to use a ball-peen hammer to form a rivet. This method has less control than a cross-peen, but it is probably a little faster. Drop the hammer so it falls near the outside edge of the rivet end. Continue around the wire, then strike a few blows in the center. Repeat until the rivet head forms.

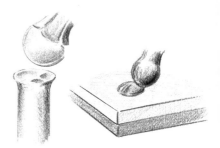

Starting with a Taper

It's possible to match the diameter of a drill bit with the diameter of wire by measuring carefully or by drilling a test hole in a piece of scrap metal. If you don't have a perfect match, use this method to guarantee a snug fit. Choose a piece of wire that is larger than the hole you have made. File a gradual taper along the last half inch of the wire until it slides into the hole. Push it in hard, perhaps even using pliers, or driving the wire as if it were a nail. Trim to length, file the ends flat, and proceed as above.

This is a very slight taper...

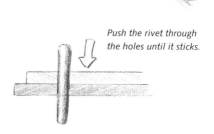

Push the rivet through the holes until it sticks.

FLUSH RIVETS (DISAPPEARING RIVETS)

Most rivets achieve their holding power because of the head that sits on top of the outermost sheets. If this head was cut off, the rivet would be reduced to a metal rod and there would be no permanent connection between the parts. In the variation called a flush rivet, the parts being joined are prepared with a funnel-shaped depression that holds the swell in the end of the wire. When excess metal is filed away, there still remains a portion of rivet head below the surface. If this is a contrasting color, it will appear as an inlaid dot. If the same metal is used for the rivet and the base, the rivet disappears.

To make the chamfer, or counter-sunk recess, first drill the hole that will hold the rivet. Use a larger drill bit, simply held in your hand, and rotate it a few turns in the hole. In most cases, a small recess is enough to make a surprisingly strong rivet.

1 Drill holes as described above (all in one piece, one in the other pieces).

2 Use a larger drill bit to carve a chamfer around the inside edge of the hole. Don't use a drill because you might go too far; just spin the large bit in your fingers. You can make flush rivets on one or both ends of a rivet.

3 Insert a tight-fitting annealed wire. Snip to length, file flat, and tap as before, working on both ends until the rivet head is formed and lays flat on the surface.

4 File or grind the exposed rivet head away. Finish in a way that is consistent with the rest of the piece.

NAILHEAD RIVETS

This variation starts by forming a ball or cap on a rivet before it is inserted into the assembly. It is recommended for situations where
• the head will not be accessible for hammering
• the material being joined is flexible and therefore requires a larger rivet head (fabric, leather, rubber, etc.)
• as a design enhancement

1 Draw a bead on the end of a piece of wire by holding it vertically into a torch flame. Focus the heat just above the bottom tip of the wire until it starts to melt. At this point the metal will draw itself into a sphere and start to crawl up the wire. Silver and gold lend themselves to this very well. Copper, brass, and nickel silver work best with a very hot torch. Whatever the metal, withdraw the heat slowly when the ball is the proper size. If you take the torch away abruptly, the outer surface of the sphere will wrinkle like a raisin because of the different cooling rates between the inside and outside of the ball. By slowly pulling the flame away, this difference is removed and the sphere will harden with a smooth surface.

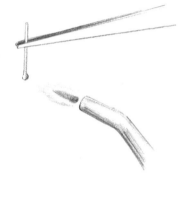

2 To make a nail heading die, drill a hole the same diameter as the rivet wire, or slightly larger into a piece of steel or thick brass. As a convenience for future use, it is helpful to make a plate with a range of holes. Alternately, you can use a round drawplate—work from the front, so you are not pressing the nail head into the tapered drawing hole. Set the heading die across the open jaws of a vise or the hardy hole of an anvil and slide the wire into place.

3 Strike the wire with a planishing hammer to form a nail head. As required by the design, you might ornament this head by directional hammering, stamping, or filing.

4 Remove the rivet from the die and continue as described above. In this case, one head is already formed, so hammering will be done on only one end.

Shaping and Finishing Rivets

In many cases, careful hammering with a polished hammer face leaves a neatly formed and attractive rivet head. Light work with sandpaper or a pumice wheel is usually all that is required to finish the rivet. In some cases, additional ornamental work with files, burs, or gravers is used to embellish the rivet head.

To make a neatly symmetrical dome, especially in a production situation, make or purchase a beading tool. This is a steel rod with a polished depression in the end. They are sold as a stonesetting tool, where they are used to shape and polish the tips of prongs. These are small, and unfortunately, they are often too small for the rivets I make. To make my own beading tools, I cut the head off a common nail and mount it into a flex shaft or drill press. Hold a ball bur in a pin vise to cut a bowl-shaped depression in the end of the nail. It is important that

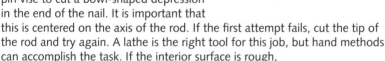

this is centered on the axis of the rod. If the first attempt fails, cut the tip of the rod and try again. A lathe is the right tool for this job, but hand methods can accomplish the task. If the interior surface is rough, it should be cleaned with abrasive wheels. These can be shaped by holding them against a file—sculpt the rubber grinding wheel into a sphere, then run it inside the concave tip. Continue until the shape is smooth and bright.

Make a rivet in any of the ways described above, then mount the beading tool in a drill press or flex shaft. Touch the tip of the tool into a light oil for lubrication, and run the tool at a medium speed on the tip of the rivet. Apply enough pressure to burnish the rivet head, but be careful that you are not damaging the area around the rivet.

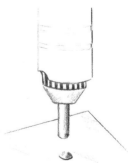

BLIND RIVETS

A blind rivet is sort of like a nail head rivet except that the nail head is replaced by a larger element. Picture a thumbtack, then make the head of the tack into an ornamental design element and you have the idea.

1 Make the "cap" or face piece of the rivet. This can be done through fabrication, overlay, roll printing, casting, or with metal clay.

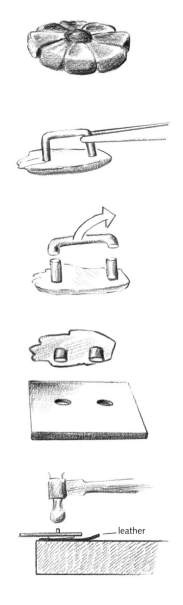

2 Solder a length of wire onto the backside of the rivet caps. Cut a length of wire at least four times as long as the pins, and bend it into a "U" in which the two vertical arms are parallel and even. Apply flux, premelt solder onto the tips of the wire, then hold the wire in place as you heat the cap. After soldering and pickling, snip off the center portion to leave two legs. File the tips flat and even.

3 To locate the rivet holes, put a bit of paint, ink, or typewriter correction fluid on the tips and lower the cap into position. Centerpunch these dots, then drill.

4 Assemble the elements, insert the legs of the blind rivet, and form the rivet heads as before.

—leather

Rotating Elements

There are times when a rivet is used to attach parts that are intended to rotate or pivot. The best way to make a loose rivet is to add a layer in the assembly that can be removed. Before the rivet head is made, insert a thin sheet of brass or nickel silver into the assembly. The size will depend on the scale of the work, but a typical size is about a half-inch wide and a couple inches long. Cut a narrow "V" into the thin end, and slide this so it encompasses the rivet. Make the rivet as usual, tapping the pin until the heads on each end are well formed. Pull the sheet out and rotate the parts until they are moving freely. Add a drop of light oil if necessary.

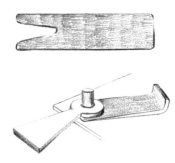

Non-Rotating Elements

When you don't want parts to rotate, the easiest solution is usually to use two or more rivets. In cases where that is not desirable, either build an invisible stop in the underside or arrange a stop outside the piece as part of the design.

Depending on the materials in the piece, it might be possible to raise stitches on the underside of the cap of a rivet (or the piece being riveted). These small burs, which are raised with a graver, will be pressed into the layer beneath as the rivet locks the parts together. While this solution is subtle, in many cases it will be sufficient to lock the parts in place.

To create a stronger version of the same thing, solder a pin onto the back of the piece and drill a hole into the layer below that lines up with it. Again, the completion of the riveting process will lock the parts into a non-rotating position.

TUBE RIVETS

When a rivet is made from a tube rather than a solid pin, the swelling at the ends is created not by upsetting, but by curling the lip of the tube outward. The advantages of a tube rivet are that they involve little or no pounding, they use less material, and they are, well, tubes. The opening through the rivet makes it possible to thread a chain, a thong, an earwire, or a dangle through the piece (to name only a few options).

1 As before, the holes at both ends of the stack to be assembled must make a tight fit on the rivet. If this fit is loose, extra effort and material will be needed, just to reach the edge. Make the hole as tight as possible, so the tube slides on only with effort. If the hole is too large, forge the metal around the hole with a ball peen hammer against steel to coax the metal inward.

2 Cut a length of tubing a bit longer than will be needed to reach through the assembly. Anneal the tube. Note that almost all tubing—sterling, gold, copper, and brass—is sold in a hard condition. The simple step of annealing can be the difference between success and failure.

3 Slide the tube into place so one end extends between one and two millimeters beyond the top surface. Cut off or file the other end so the same amount projects there. Sand the edges to make them clean and smooth—they will not be as easy to reach after they have been curled over.

4 Insert a blunt round tool into the end of the tube and pull it outward. Tilt the tool to the opposite side and do it again. Repeat two more times, at points midway between the first two. In some ways this can seem like the inverse of setting a bezel. Flip the stack over and repeat on the other end. After doing this, the tube should be at least lightly tacked in place.

5 To smooth out the waves and simultaneously continue to curl the metal outward, you need a tool

with a blunt cone. This might be found on a commercial nail set, or you can simply file the desired shape on the end of a steel rod like a nail or a bolt. While not mandatory, it's best to have two of these. Set one vertically in a vise (or have someone hold it upright on a solid table) and set the tube rivet on it. With the other tool on the top of the stack, tap lightly. Since the upper surface receives more of the blow than the lower one (don't ask), flip the piece over periodically.

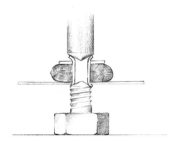

6 This step is optional, or it may be done in lieu of Step #8. In other words, some people do this and others don't. Try it to see if it works for you. Set the tools aside, and rest the rivet on a solid surface. Tap the edges of the rivet with a small ball-peen hammer or dapping punch to complete the curl and smooth out the surface.

7 Finish the rivet head with sandpaper, a pumice wheel, and polishing tools.

Variation

• To create a tube rivet that requires almost no force, cut slots into the upper edge of the tube. I suggest at least six openings, or three slices with a saw. These must all be cut to the same depth. Bend these outward with pliers, working on one end before the tube is inserted. To make this same closure on the other end, cut slots down to the surface level and press a pointed tool or a small dapping punch into the end of the tubes. The legs will splay out and can be pressed down with a dowel or with pliers.

CUTLERS' RIVETS

These ingenious rivets have been used for years to attach knife handles onto blades (hence the name). They offer secure joints with little stress on the parts, and have the added advantage of making large or ornamented heads very easy to create. Cutlers rivets are sold by knifemaking supply companies in a limited range of sizes and materials, but they are not difficult for a jeweler to make.

1 A rivet set includes two parts: a solid pin and a short length of tubing, each attached to a disk. These can be made of sterling, copper, brass, or nickel, or almost any other metal. The diameter of the solid rod must be slightly larger than the inside diameter of the tube. Bigger but only *slightly* bigger. The connection depends on the friction of this rod against the inner walls of the tube when the parts are pressed together.

2 Solder the pin and the tube to the backside of the rivet heads. These parts usually match (for instance as they appear on a knife handle), but there is nothing functional that requires this. Pickle, clean, and polish the parts.

3 Drill a hole in the parts to be assembled that is very slightly larger than the outside of the tube. When the parts are joined, the tube will swell just a little bit. If the material is flexible it will absorb this, but if it is not, this small pressure might be enough to crack the parts being joined.

4 Set the parts temporarily together and hold them up to the assembly to check the length. The pin needs to be far enough into the tube to lock into place, but this is usually accomplished with only a millimeter or two of friction cut to length, if needed. File a slight bevel on the tip of the rod; this will help it "find" the tube when the parts slide together.

5 When you are sure that all the components are ready (it's difficult to undo a cutlers' rivet), put the parts in position and squeeze the rivet. This can be done by hammering the rivet, but I prefer the slow and more controlled squeeze accomplished by a screwing action. I set the stack into the jaws of a vise and slowly close the jaws until the rivet heads are snug against the facing layers. If the rivet heads are ornamented or have a contour, protect them with a layer of leather or rubber.

Variations

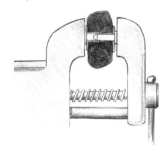

- In especially tall assemblies, it might be easier to solder pins onto both parts and join them with a length of tubing.

- Cutlers' rivets are usually solid, but the entire structure can be made of tubing if you need an opening through the connection.

POP Rivets

This is a patented device that makes it possible (in fact easy) to set rivets from one side. The concept is ingenious. Start with something that looks like a tube rivet with a head built onto one end. Insert into this something that looks like a nail, but that has a weak spot strategically placed in its shank. This piece is inserted into a gun-shaped tool that works a bit like a stapler in reverse. Slide the POP Rivet into a hole drilled in the pieces to be joined, and squeeze the lever. The tool grips the nail and pulls it out through the tube. The head of the nail swells the end of the tube, and at a specific pressure the shaft snaps.

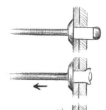
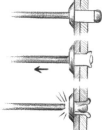

1 Slide the rivet into the hole and insert the pin in the driver.

2 As the driver pulls the pin out, the rivet starts to bulge.

3 When sufficient force is applied, the pin snaps off.

Pop rivets are made in a variety of styles, sizes, and metals, including aluminum and copper. The simple hand device is appropriate for studio use, but electric and pneumatic versions are also available.

WASHERS

We're all familar with a washer—a flat steel disk with a hole in the middle. Except for putting them where the instructions say when we're assembling a trike or a barbeque grill, we probably don't give them much thought. We should.

Washers are the unsung heroes of cold connections. In a rigid material like metal, the relatively small bulge of a rivet head is enough to make a strong joint, but imagine a rivet in a flexible material like rubber, leather, or fabric. The largest rivet head you can form will quickly pull through and the parts would separate. Now we see the genius of a washer.

Technically, there is not much to say about using washers, other than to point out that you add it to the stack before completing the cold connection. All varieties of rivets, tabs, and screws can

accept a washer. For a good look and ease in assembly, the hole in the rivet should make a tight fit on the rivet wire or tube.

The job that a washer does, to enlarge the holding power of a rivet head, has nothing to do with its shape or the ornamentation (or lack of it). And bear in mind that a single washer can handle two or more rivets. The possiblities are endless.

Nonmetal Washers

The purpose of a washer is to contain a flexible material inside the cold connection of a rivet or a threaded joint. While metal is an obvious choice, it is not the only choice. Use any material that can be given the appropriate shape, drilled with an appropriate hole, and that is significantly more rigid than the parts being joined. Examples of possible washer materials include plastic, vinyl (e.g., old records), hardwood, and even glass.

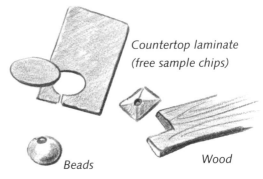

Countertop laminate (free sample chips)

Beads

Wood

MISCELLANEOUS COLD CONNECTIONS

One of the most exciting elements of cold connections is their amazing pervasiveness. Wherever you look, you can find a point of connection that offers opportunity for modification. Look around the kitchen, the hardware store, and the backyard, and you'll see ways that nature and people have figured out ways to put parts together. This information, combined with your personal vision and immediate needs, will open the door to all sorts of new ideas.

Lashing & Knots

Perhaps the very first method used to hold parts together was to tie them with a strand of fiber. We see remnants of this technology in the way stone points were attached to spears and arrow shafts, and we can easily imagine the way similar constructions were used to make lodgings and tools.

Sailor's Knotwork

How to create a research lab in lashing: Take many groups of men, put them in isolation on a wooden boat, give them almost unlimited amounts of rope, and set them the task of keeping lots of parts together under a wide variety of conditions. In other words, create the principal transportation industry of the 17th and 18th century.

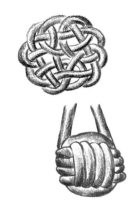

There are books available that describe the rich inventory of knotwork developed by the world's sailors. Even better, visit one of the many museums of maritime history where you can see examples yourself.

Asian Knotwork

Another resource for lashing information is an investigation of Japanese, Chinese, and Korean knotwork. In addition to a similar history of using cords for functional purposes, Japanese artists developed knotwork into a highly organized and structured art form. Of course you might want to start by duplicating these knots for their own beauty, but remain open to ways the sensibilities of the Japanese craftsmen can influence your own use of lashing.

Spring-Loaded Connections

This family is large, and no doubt, it gets larger every month. The general idea is that parts fit together and are then joined, permanently or temporarily, when an element that is triggered by a spring locks it into place. Here are a few familiar examples:

Umbrella

You know this one—when you open an umbrella, a tubular sleeve travels along the shaft until it reaches the top, the point where the ribs of the umbrella are fully expanded. At that point, a wing of metal snaps out from inside the shaft to lock into the sleeve and hold it in position. In this example, the wing-shaped hook is large enough that we can press it back into the shaft and reverse the process, but it would be easy to make this connection more permanent, simply by making the wing small enough that it wouldn't project out from the sleeve.

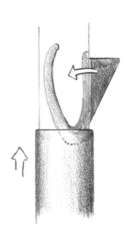

Watchband Pin

This familiar joining mechanism also shows up in a larger version in the bathroom, where it is used to hold a roll of paper. The pin consists of a tube and a wire (or second tube) that fits neatly inside it. The two parts are cut to the appropriate length and capped on one end. A small coil spring is inserted in the tube and the parts are slid together. To engage the connection, compress the parts, then fit the ends into sockets in the receiving element. When the spring expands, the rod is locked into place. To make this joining method permanent, or nearly so, make the sockets deep and the surface of the tube smooth. With nothing to grip, the pin will be very difficult to remove.

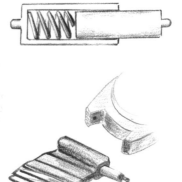

Rubber Bands

It's difficult to go through a day without encountering a rubber band. They are used to keep our newspapers tidy, to hold stacks of mail together, to bundle vegetables at the grocery, and in countless other uses. When we think of rubberbands as lightweight loops of soft rubber in these familiar sizes, it is difficult to imagine their use in jewelry or metalwork. But think again.

I remember being surprised, years ago, when I looked under my car and discovered that the muffler was held in place with a rubber band. Of course the rubber was tough, and the band was a four-inch loop of quarter-inch strapping. Still, there it was. And at the other end of the spectrum, anyone who has worn dental braces will remember the tiny rubber bands that came with that enterprise. Here we not only have an example, but also a scale that starts to look possible for jewelry. For stronger rubber, investigate commercial O-rings, which are available at hardware stores.

At the other end of the spectrum, when you're looking for small and delicate rubber bands, you can create them by cutting off pieces of a rubber glove.

Spiral Coils

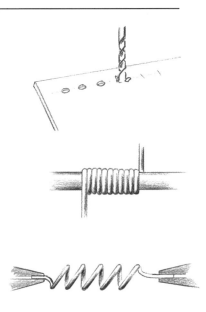

We've all seen spiral notebooks, but we don't usually think of the expanded coil of wire as a cold connection. It is, though, and the same idea can be used in many different ways. Drill equally spaced holes in the parts to be joined. The holes need to be about half again larger in diameter than the thickness of the wire if you want the parts to move freely. Wind a length of wire around a round mandrel, laying each loop tight against the preceding one to create a tidy coil. Grab the coil at each end with pliers and pull in opposite directions to expand the spiral. This is often enough to make a uniform structure, but if greater precision is needed, find a piece of metal, wood, or plastic with a thickness that matches the desired spacing between coils. Force this in to the coil, then screw the two pieces against one another.

Snaps

Snaps depend on friction, usually coupled with a slight spring action. Consider the common snap that is used on jackets, jeans, and watchbands. Usually a shallow cup is forced over a similarly shallow tube, with enough force that the two parts become stuck together. Note that if this is all that happens, every time the parts are pressed together, a small amount of metal will be rubbed off or bent. This will make each closure less secure than the last, and there will come a time when the parts won't stay together.

The solution is to create a way that one element has a little give, either to contract (the smaller, internal element) or to expand (the cap, or outer element). This subtle concept uses the ability of metal (and plastic) to move, then bounce back to its original shape. This can often be as simple as a slot cut into the part—experiment to find the stress release that is appropriate for the shape of your snap.

It's also important that the closed clasp have a "rest" position. That is, the tension of the clasp should be greatest midway when the parts are brought together, but then the tension should relax. This is usually done by having a rim or bulge at one place. If the walls of the two elements are always rubbing against each other, the clasp will be stiff and the mechanism will wear out quickly. If the parts go through a tension point and then relax, the parts are no longer under tension, so wear is reduced. Also, when the parts of the clasp are past the tension point, they are more likely to stay in this position. That is, it takes some effort to undo the clasp.

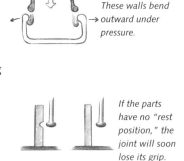

These walls bend outward under pressure.

If the parts have no "rest position," the joint will soon lose its grip.

Reversible Connections Made Permanent

A reversible connection is something that comes together and can be taken apart—a clasp on a necklace or a bracelet, for instance. In most cases, these depend on the ability of metal to flex and return to the original shape, and in most cases, precise measurements are what make the connection function. A whole realm of possiblities opens when we consider modifying these connections so they snap together, then stay together. Imagine a box clasp without a trigger and you get the idea.

There are a gazillion kinds of fasterners like this, and several thousand are in current use by auto makers. Jewelers and workers in small metals are in a perfect position to understand the workings of reversible connections, then to adjust them to the specific needs of a piece.

Part Two
Hot Connections

OVERVIEW

It should be remembered that in the early days of metalworking, the people who made metal were also responsible for smelting it and transforming rough ingots into workable stock. These processes depend on the use of heat and an understanding of the properties of molten metal, so it is not surprising that the ability to fuse and solder metal parts together is as ancient as metalworking itself.

TYPE	METALS	TOOLS	STRENGTH
Soft Soldering	Copper, brass, pewter, sterling, tinplate, & others	Soldering iron or small torch	So-so. Surface area is critical to make a strong joint.
Silver Brazing (silver soldering)	Gold and silver alloys, copper, brass, nickel silver, & others	Torch	Very strong when done properly. It is important to create deep penetration through proper heating.
Spot Welding Fusion	Gold and silver alloys, copper, brass, nickel silver, titanium	Electric welder ("Sparkie" is a popular brand)	Strong but localized. Typically the joints are very small.
Welding Forge Torch Arc	Iron, steel, platinum, aluminum	Coal forge Oxy-fuel torch Electric welder	Very strong; same as the parent metal
Laser	Gold and silver alloys, copper, brass, nickel silver	Solid state laser welding machine	Reported to be three times stronger than soldering

SOFT SOLDERING

In this method, a low melting alloy is used to join parts together. This bond relies on the adhesive ability of alloys that melt at a low temperature. Soft soldering is used in copper plumbing, stained glass, and some jewelry construction.

Advantages
- Low heat means that usually the parts do not warp, anneal, or oxidize.
- Equipment is simple.
- Can be used on a wide variety of metals.
- Relatively low cost.
- Because there is little or no oxidation, cleanup is quick.

Disadvantages
- Joint is not as strong as brazing.
- Except in the case of pewter, the solder cannot be fully blended in.
- Because of the relatively low melting point, soft soldering cannot be used where the finished object will be under high heat.
- In some cases, soft solder alloys can stain clothes or present a health risk. This is solved by selecting the proper alloy.
- When soft solder is heated to brazing temperatures, it penetrates and corrodes precious metal.

Steps for Soft Soldering

1 Clean all parts of oil, paint, graphite, etc. If possible, slightly roughen the surface with sandpaper, Scotch-Brite, or pumice.

2 Apply the appropriate flux to all parts.

3 Preheat the metal to melt the flux.

4 Apply solder, then continue heating in such a way that all the parts reach the flow point of the solder at the same time.

5 As the melting temperature of the solder is reached, reduce the heat (for instance by lifting the torch slightly) and allow the work to soak at heat until the solder flows. Allow the work to sit undisturbed until the solder hardens.

6 Quench in water and wash with soap to remove flux residue.

Equipment

Soldering Irons

For many years, the standard tool for soft soldering consisted of a heavy copper bar attached to a steel rod that was fitted with a wooden handle. This tool, called a copper, was heated in a gas ring or kiln, then held against the parts to heat them to the proper temperature. Typically, a soldering station would keep two or three coppers in a fire so that as one cooled, another would be warming up. These have been largely replaced by electric soldering guns.

Soldering Guns and Irons

These now-familiar tools use an electrical current to heat a wire that in turn, melts the solder. As current is passed through a wire of specific thickness, heat is produced. This flow can be regulated with a pressure switch (like a trigger) or with a dial rheostat. The shape of the heat tip can be modified to suit various needs. In some models, the tips are attached to threaded rods, which makes them easy to interchange, and to create unique tips in the studio from standard bolts.

Pen

This miniature version of an electric soldering iron replaces electricity from a wall plug with current from a battery. They are limited in the temperatures that can be achieved and the length of time they can be used, but for small work, the increased ease of handling is an advantage.

Torches

Almost any torch can be used for soft soldering because the melting temperatures of these alloys are so low. Any jewelers torch can be used, as can the small butane torches sold for household repair and kitchen use. For someone on a budget, these offer the appealing advantage of low cost and great versatility. For very small work, even the simple torches that use a butane lighter will work.

Work Area

Because soft solder flows at relatively low temperatures (typically under 500° F, 260° C), very little special equipment is needed. It is best to work on a heatproof surface, such as ceramic tiles, concrete, or linoleum. Excess solder and flux can make the work area a bit messy, so it is helpful if the work surface can be easily wiped down.

Here are a few miscellaneous supplies for the soldering area:

- a few pieces of fire brick
- a couple large bolts or similar pieces of steel to weight pieces into position
- large tweezers
- small tweezers
- inexpensive disposable flux brushes
- a small rag to wipe off excess flux
- a stand to hold the soldering iron safely off the surface. This will keep the tip clean and help prevent it from cooling quickly.
- various clips, commercial and handmade, to hold parts together while soldering

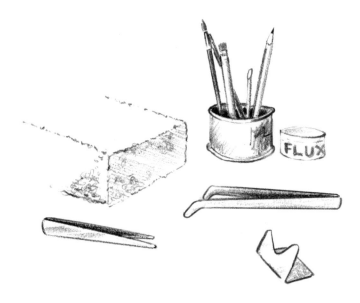

Lead/Tin Solder

The most common alloy used for soft soldering is an alloy of lead and tin, two low-melting gray-colored metals, both soft enough to be scratched with a fingernail. The eutectic alloy consists of 37% tin and 63% lead and is cleverly called 37/63 Solder. This mixture has the distinction of shifting from solid to liquid (and back again) almost immediately. To say it another way, some alloys will exist in a semi-liquid or slushy state—a temperature at which they are neither fully melted nor fully solid. In the case of this alloy, that zone is so small that it appears that the solder goes from liquid to solid instantly.

This property is convenient when you are holding parts together manually—you want the joint to harden before your hand trembles and moves the part. Of course there might be times when you want a few seconds to slide parts into their proper position, and for those cases you will prefer 30/70 solder, an alloy that contains slightly less tin. The gap between liquid and solid is large enough to allow a few seconds of working time.

Tin/Silver Solder

For many years, lead-bearing solder was used to attach silver handles to nickel or steel knife blades, and to seal copper pipes in refrigerators. When society became aware of the health risk of lead poisoning, metallurgists devised new solders that combine similar ease and low working temperature. These solders contain 90-97% tin and 3-10% silver. They are available under several trade names, such as TIX, Sta-Brite, and TinSilver4, and Castin. They usually require their own flux (typically a clear solution that contains zinc chloride and ammonium chloride), which is often sold in the same package. These solders can be handled the same way as the lead/tin alloys described above. The same soldering tools can be used for the two types of solder, but the tips should be filed to remove one type when changing over to the other.

Other Solders

While it is true that solders generally divide into two families (soft solder and brazing alloys), it would be misleading to imply that the situation is this clear. There are a number of proprietary solder alloys that fall in between the two larger groups. These are typically active in range of 900°–1200° F (480°–650° C). They are widely used in industry, and can be very useful for studio artists too. These solders combine the best of both worlds—they are often as strong as silver brazing alloys, and yet they can fill a gap more like soft solder. Some brands are specifically designed to work well on cast iron and oxidized stainless steel, all problematic situations. Because each of these solders has its own benefits and requirements, and because new alloys are frequently introduced, readers are directed to the Internet for the latest information. Some suppliers and their sites are given in the Appendix.

PURE METALS

These are the metals that are most commonly used to create low-melting solders. They are similar in many ways: they are white or gray, have relatively low melting points, are soft, and by themselves generally have poor working properties. By combining these metals in various proportions, a wide range of solder alloys can be made. The chart at the bottom of the page gives details on just a few of the dozens of possibilities.

metal	symbol	° C	°F
Antimony	Sb	631	1168
Bismuth	Bi	271	520
Cadmium	Cd	321	610 (health hazard)
Lead	Pb	327	621
Tin	Sn	323	450
Zinc	Zn	419	786

SOFT SOLDER ALLOYS

There are many options for low-melting solder alloys, some specifically formulated for certain metals, applications, or color matches. Consult welding and plumbing supply companies or the Web. In most cases, it is wise to buy the recommended flux from the same source to insure compatibility.

Pb	Sn	Ag	Sb	° C	° F
	96	4		221	430
	95		5	240	464
10	90			213	415
30	70			193	380
37	63			257	495 (eutectic)
40	60			190	365
50	50			215	420
60	40			238	460

FLUX

Important Note: Fluxes used for soft solders are quite different from those used for silver brazing. The fluxes described here are designed for low temperature soldering; they will burn away long before the flow point of silver solder.

Liquid Flux

In bygone days, plumbers, glaziers, and tinsmiths made their own flux, usually by dissolving zinc in hydrochloric acid. This process rendered the acid less dangerous, which lead them to call the mixture "killed acid." The method still works, of course, but nowadays most people purchase the flux ready to use. It is sold as a clear, almost odorless liquid. Despite the earlier description, the solution is still corrosive and should be stored and handled with care. Wash your hands after using it, and avoid getting it in your eyes or mouth. If that happens, rinse well and call a doctor.

zin

Paste Flux

This variation combines the liquid described above with petroleum jelly to create a gooey paste that can be brushed on surfaces to be soldered. The effect is the same; the benefit is that this version lends itself to situations where the watery flux would be difficult to apply.

Flux Core

In an effort to make soft soldering as easy as possible, manufacturers developed a tubular solder that has its flux inside. The use is exactly the same as the other solders except that you don't need to apply flux as a separate step. This is also known as rosin core, Solu-Core, and Clean-Core, the latter using organic fluxes that are easy to remove after soldering.

Preparation

This is perhaps the most important step in soft soldering. A well-prepared joint is clean, tight, stable, and accessible. Or, to say it another way, if you want to make soldering a protracted and frustrating experience, make a sloppy joint with wiggly parts, and see that it has a film of oil.

1 Use steel wool or Scotch-Brite to clean all parts thoroughly just before you are ready to solder. Even the tarnish that forms over a few hours is sufficient to cause problems. Apply a thin coating of flux to the parts before assembling them.

2 If possible, lock the parts together. The very best way uses the parts themselves, for instance, with tabs, integrated staples, or crimped flanges. This is economical of material and does not introduce heat sinks. Second best is to use clamps, but because these will draw heat away from the parts being soldered, be conservative. Use paper clips, bulldog clamps, hairpins, or studio-made equivalents.

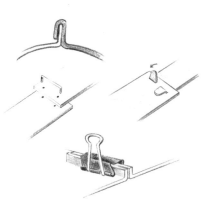

3 Set the work on a soldering surface in a way that allows you to have 360-degree access with the torch or soldering iron. This could be a matter of working on the corner of a counter or positioning the workpiece on a turntable. Either way, avoid the temptation to use elaborate props to balance complicated parts. It is frustrating to have a house of cards tumble down, especially when it happens just as the solder starts to flow.

Soldering with a Torch

This method is especially preferred when the solder seams are long, such as when joining large sheets, or pipes. Soldering is best when the flow is a single continuous action, and this requires that relatively large portions of the metal be kept hot. This is not possible with a soldering iron.

In many cases, it is most efficient to feed the solder directly from the spool into the joint. The trick to making this work is to direct the heat onto the workpiece rather than the solder. Let heat from the object melt the solder.

In other cases, it makes more sense to lay bits of solder into place before applying heat. This has the advantage of putting the right amount in the right place, and of freeing a hand to hold parts or make delicate adjustments. When using this method, flatten the round solder wire by hammering it before cutting it into small pieces. These flat chips are less likely to roll away than the small cylinders created by clipping off bits of wire.

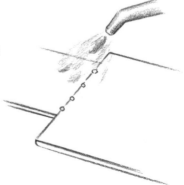

The Soldering Process

If the parts are well-fitted (and they are, right?), only a small amount of solder is needed. A piece the size of a grain of rice should fill an inch of a seam. It is usually easier to add more solder later than to remove excess.

Use a soft, bushy flame. Soft solder flows at about one-fourth the temperature of silver solders, so people who are used to brazing find it easy to overheat when soft soldering. Use a gentle flame, hold it several inches away from the metal, and keep it moving. If the flux starts to smoke, the metal is too hot. Stay alert for this signal, and pull the torch away immediately if you see smoke.

Heat should travel from the workpiece to the solder. Heat the metal, distributing the flame so that all the parts being soldered will reach the same temperature at the same time. This means that thick or large pieces need to be heated longer than small ones. As soon as the solder pieces start to lose their shape, lift the torch to reduce the heat. The goal is to maintain an even temperature as the heat already present diffuses through the metal.

It is possible to manipulate solder flow, but bear in mind that this risks bumping parts out of position. To guide solder along a seam, use a chopstick, a bamboo skewer, or a bit of fiberglas insulation. The trick is to touch the solder only when it is molten; too soon and you are pushing solid metal around, too late and the solder has hardened in its new position. You can reheat and try to move it around, but this is a little tricky.

When the solder flows, remove the heat but do not test the joint. The workpiece will hold its heat for a while, and this keeps the solder fluid. It is very frustrating to make a lovely joint, then mess it up by picking up the parts too soon. Allow the piece to sit undisturbed for several minutes before gingerly testing the joint. While it is possible to hasten cooling by splashing water on the joint, I don't recommend it because it risks making the joint brittle.

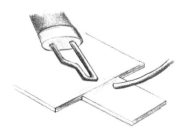

Soldering with an Iron

As described above, clean all parts and bend them so they fit together neatly. Apply an appropriate flux. Note that some solder has flux contained inside, and in these cases, additional solder might not be necessary (but it almost never hurts).

• Turn the iron on (or depress the trigger) and give the tool at least a minute to heat up. Press the tip of a hot soldering iron firmly onto the joint, touching both parts to be joined, if possible. Allow at least 30 seconds for heat to transfer from the iron to the metal, then touch the end of a piece of solder wire to the joint. Alternatively, and especially in delicate areas, clip a small piece of solder and lay it in place with tweezers.

- If the work piece is hot enough, the solder will flow as soon as it touches the metal, which is what you want. When that happens, slide the tip aside to allow the solder to penetrate the joint. If the solder does not flow, continue pressing the iron against the metal. If prolonged contact doesn't work, it is possible that your soldering iron just doesn't deliver enough heat to raise the metal to the necessary temperature.

- As with other soldering methods, resist the urge to move the piece too soon. It can take almost a minute for the solder to harden.

- Once the solder has hardened and you can hold the piece in your hand, it is OK to quench it in water. Use a rag or paper towel to wipe off as much of the sticky flux residue as you can. Following that, use a strong soap or kitchen cleanser like Comet or Copper-Brite to wash off the rest. Avoid using steel wool or Scotch-Brite at this stage because they just get clogged up and messy.

Cool Heat

Cool Heat is a patented tool that uses batteries and microcircuitry to produce a brief instant burst of heat at a localize  spot. The name comes from the fact that the heat dissipates in a few seconds. The tool is compact, elegant and inexpensive. It was designed for very small scale work, for instance in creating electronic circuitry. In this context it works well, but as the instructions make clear, the tool will not work for pieces of metal much heavier than fine wires, even with the larger, professional-duty tool.

BRAZING
Description & Concept

A simple description of the difference between soldering and brazing is that brazing takes place at higher temperatures and yields bonds of greater strength. If that's enough for you, leave it there. For those who want to probe deeper, though, let's examine what happens at higher temperatures, and why this makes brazing stronger than soldering.

Metals are made up of crystals, which we can think of as bricks (very very tiny, rather oddly shaped bricks, but let's keep it simple). When metal is heated, it expands, which is to say that the bricks move apart. The higher the heat, the more the bricks move and the larger the spaces between them. There comes a point where they are so far apart they lose attraction for each other and the sample melts. In brazing we create an alloy called solder that becomes molten just when the spaces between crystals is largest. At that moment, molten solder is pulled into the microscopic spaces between crystals through osmosis, just as water droplets are pulled into the spaces of a sponge or paper towel.

A microscopic view of metal at room temperature.

If the solder has similar color and working properties to the parent metal, and if all the parts soaked up solder to the same degree, the resulting bond is very much like the metal around it. It is invisible to the naked eye, will bend, file, and color like the parent metal, and it will be as strong. Brazing has been the primary joining method for goldsmiths for at least 5000 years, which is a testament not only to its longevity but to the absolutely wonderful results that can be achieved with it.

The following pages describe in detail the equipment, preparation, and process of silver brazing. Before wading into the specifics, it might be helpful to see the whole process at a glance. The next page is a map for beginners and a review for people with brazing experience.

When heated, the crystals move apart, creating spaces.

THE BRAZING PROCESS

As described earlier, brazing is a matter of developing sufficient heat to create microscopic spaces between crystals, then introducing a fluid alloy, while all the time keeping the metal free of oxides. Here are the cardinal rules for the process, which is usually called silver soldering. The following pages describe each of these in greater detail.

1 The metal must be clean and the parts must fit together very well. Generally I try to avoid props, but sometimes it is helpful to use locking tweezers, wire, or clamps to hold pieces in position.

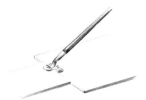

2 Apply flux around the joint. Some metalsmiths also apply a protective layer to minimize internal oxidation.

3 Either place solder onto the joint, or prepare to introduce solder by probe or wire during the heating process.

4 Heat in such a way that the parts reach the flow temperature of the solder at the same time.

5 When soldering is complete, clean the work in pickle or with a mild abrasive like household cleaner.

TORCHES

Torches are not the most important component in soldering, but almost. In museums we can see fantastic gold objects made centuries ago with charcoal and oil lamps, which prove that skill is the Number One component, regardless of equipment. That said, the better the torch, the easier it is to solder well. So, what's the best torch?

The answer depends on the work being done. This is easiest to answer when there is a single scale and material. Choosing the best torch for a person who spends all day, every day retipping prongs on gold rings is relatively easy. In many cases though, the choice of a best torch is a compromise that will meet a wide range of needs.

Torches can be easily divided into two families; those that use oxygen from the atmosphere and those that use bottled oxygen. The former are cheaper to buy and maintain, while the latter deliver hotter and smaller flames. Because about 80% of the atmosphere is nitrogen, which has no bearing on flames, torches that depend on the oxygen that exists around us need to push a lot of extra gas through the nozzle. This limits the heat that can be produced and the compression of the flame. On the bright side, it means you'll never run out of oxygen (or, if you do, you've got bigger problems than soldering).

Atmosphere Torches

air in here

Atmosphere torches are easy to recognize because they have only one valve. The fuel gas, typically propane, butane, or acetylene, is under pressure in a tank. When you open the valve, the gas hisses out, just like air tries to escape from a balloon when you open the neck. Holes in the torch nozzle suck air into the tube as the gas rushes past—more gas draws more air. The air and gas mix in the torch tip and come out at the end in an ideally burnable combination. The size and placement of the holes has been carefully engineered to insure a perfect mixture. As you open the valve to let more gas escape, the gas pulls more air along with it, which means the mixture is self-regulating. In some cases the air supply is passive and in others the air is pushed into the torch with a bellows, a blowpipe, or a compressor.

Because of this automatic feature, atmosphere torches are excellent for beginners. They are commonly found in jewelry studios, because they provide a wide range of temperatures and flame sizes. They do it safely, economically, and in a way that is almost foolproof. Atmosphere torches are made that work with propane, butane, natural gas, MAPP, and acetylene. Of these, the last is probably the most common in the jewelry world. It is also popular with plumbers, which means that you can often find them sold (and tanks refilled) at a plumbing supply store. In fact, the acetylene/atmosphere unit is sometimes called a plumber's torch.

Oxygen Torches

Oxygen torches, by contrast, use bottles of pure oxygen to force combustion of a fuel gas. They're also equally easy to spot—there are two tanks, two regulators, and two knobs on the torch itself. Oxygen torches are made to work with propane, natural gas, acetylene, and butane. By adjusting the two knobs, you have control over the intensity, mix, and size of the flame. Because of this, these torches take a bit longer to learn, but many people consider them worth the effort.

The greatest advantage of using pure oxygen is the much hotter temperatures that can be achieved, typically half again as hot as the same fuel using atmospheric oxygen. This increases efficiency because work moves much faster. It also makes it possible to heat small objects so quickly that solder will flow before heat has time to travel through the piece. This makes jewelry repairs possible, for instance where a stone is involved.

How to Handle Torches

The following information applies to both families of torch.

1 First, get comfortable with the torch. Balance it in your hand and learn to adjust the knob with one hand. If you are right-handed, hold the torch in your left. This might feel uncomfortable at first, but there will come a time when you need to manipulate tweezers or solder with your "smart" hand, so let your off-hand take care of the torch.

2 It is not uncommon for people to be afraid of a torch. This is understandable, but it's worth getting past this hurdle. If you are nervous about using the torch, take whatever time is needed to face up to your fears. Light the torch, extinguish it, and light it again. You'll hear various popping noises, hisses, and maybe see a small burst of flame as the torch goes out. All this is normal, and once you see that none of this is threatening, you'll feel more comfortable.

3 Don't crank on the knobs. Torch valves are delicate instruments, designed to operate at a gentle touch. Use a firm pressure when closing the knobs, but not Too Firm. Stressing the knob can actually damage the delicate parts inside the valve.

4 Use a striker to make a spark. There are several versions of these, and they all use a bit of flint scraped across a rough file-like piece of steel to generate a burst of sparks. Strikers are much safer than using matches or lighters, and worth the small effort it takes to master them. Note that one of the arms is fixed to the file element and the other moves. Position your hand so your thumb presses down on the moving (flint-holding) arm.

Flints wear away and need to be replaced. Open out the arms and unscrew the flint. Replacements are available through jewelry suppliers and at local welding supply companies. In use, hold the striker below the torch tip and open the valve just enough to let some gas escape. Opening too wide sends the gas out with such force that it blows past the spark before it has time to ignite.

5 When you are finished, lift the torch off the workpiece and gently close the valve. There might be a popping sound as the small amount of gas in the torch tip burns away. This is normal. In oxygen/fuel torches, turn off the oxygen first, then close the fuel valve.

Specialty Soldering

Using a Kiln

I'm not aware of any handcrafter using this method, but it is quite common in industry. Work is prepared with flux and solder, often in the form of a paste, and placed on a conveyor belt that runs through a kiln. By determining the pace of the travel and the heat maintained in the various zones of the kiln, it is possible to solder hundreds of pieces with little handling and perfectly consistent results.

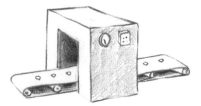

Electric Soldering

There are several variations on this technology, variably known as spot welding, tack welding, or pulse arc welding. Technically,, this is a welding rather than a brazing operation because the join does not require the addition of a solder alloy. I'll mention it here because it is often an alternative to silver soldering. The idea is that a jolt of electricity is directed at a specific location. This split-second burst of heat is sufficient to melt the metal in that specific spot. The most common use in the making of jewelry is for chains. Commercial chains are made from a specially produced wire that has a core of solder alloy. A machine forms the chain link, then two small probes come together at the joint and deliver a burst of electricity. The heat from this jolt melts the core and closes the link.

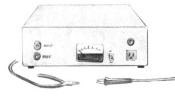

A variation on this is a type of joining done with a machine called the Sparkie. The Sparkie device is most often used to attach findings like pinstems and earring posts onto jewelry. This form of soldering cannot close a seam.

Insert a finding into the collet in the upper portion of the machine. It is important that the part to be joined has a point. The precision of this single point of contact is vital to success.

 Bring the larger unit (an earring, for instance) into contact with the tip of the finding. Though the contact generates a high temperature, it is so localized, and passes so quickly, that you can hold parts in your bare hands during this welding.

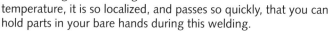

Laser Welding

One of the latest developments is laser welding, including the development of equipment at a cost and size that makes it feasible for small studios. There are several machines on the market, with more arriving each day. Because of this, readers are directed to distributors, trade fairs, and the Web to research up to date information. In a very summary way, here is how these machines work.

In a solid state laser, a beam of light is focused through a medium, which for jewelry scale, is usually a neodymium-doped yttrium aluminum garnet crystal, Nd:YAG. This beam can be controlled in its size, intensity, and duration, resulting in a pinpoint of very high temperature that allows for precise targeting of a burst of intense heat that forms and dissipates almost instantly.

In most cases, laser welding machines include a microscope and a containment area. The workpiece is set into the chamber and the site of the desired weld is lined up with crosshairs built into the microscope. A foot pedal or similar trigger is used to fire the laser, creating a welded spot instantly.

SOLDERING SURFACES

All surfaces absorb heat, and some absorb more than others. As a general rule, I prefer materials that absorb less heat because the soldering process is faster. Perhaps more important is to stick with one material. If you switch back and forth among surfaces with very different qualities, you will be forced to deal with a variable that is easily avoided.

The ideal soldering surface will reflect heat back onto the workpiece, cost almost nothing, and last forever. It will be soft enough to be shaped to hold pieces and to allow pins to be inserted as needed, but rigid enough that you can press against it. Of course nothing perfectly matches this description, but there are many materials that combine several of these qualities. The choice in the end is a personal one—try a few to see which you like best. Here are the common options, starting with the cheapest.

- Soft brick — a pottery material made for building kilns. One company calls their soft brick G-23, though other companies will have different designations. The standard size is quite large for most jewelers; I cut the bricks into fourths with a carpenters saw or a hack saw. To extend their life, wrap the brick with wire or sheet metal.

- Commercial soldering pads — these soft fibrous pads are made by pressing refractory materials together. They are generally sold in squares or rectangles about a half-inch thick, usually white.

- Pumice gravel — pumice is a naturally occuring stone created in volcanoes. Jewelry supply houses sell it in the form of light-gray gravel. Pour this into a small shallow pan. The pumice lasts forever, and it's cheap too. The disadvantage is that it doesn't provide a flat or stable surface.

- Ceramic pads — an extruded fired ceramic pad. These last a long time, but can become clogged with flux. They do not bounce...

• Charcoal — though not technically the most expensive, these top the list because they do not last as long as the others, so their cost turns out to be high. Charcoal has the dual advantages of reflecting heat best and providing a cleansing oxygen-gobbling environment. Because the charcoal catches fire each time it is used (think barbeque briquettes), it is important to extinguish the charcoal after soldering.

Heating from Below

It is also possible in some situations to avoid or minimize the role of a soldering surface by working "in thin air." An ancient way to do this is by soldering in a nest of steel wire. Here are two ways to make a nest:

Fine Wire

Pull several yards of small gauge binding wire from its spool and wad them up into a loose ball. Wrap the wire around several times as if you were making a ball of yarn. Continue wrapping and wadding to make a size that is appropriate for your work.

Thick Wire

Wrap 18–14 gauge binding wire around a cylinder like a broom handle or dowel. Pull the coil off, stretch it out, then bring the ends together and twist them to secure the loop.

Tripod

Some people like to elevate their work by placing it on a metal mesh resting on a laboratory tripod. This allows room to position the torch below the work. The advantage is that it allows better viewing of the work while soldering. Disadvantages are that it is slower (because the mesh is a heat sink), and it is possible to overheat because you cannot see the area directly affected by the flame.

THE SOLDERING STATION

For people who take a jewelry class, the first experience of a soldering area is typically a fireproof enclosure that looks like a library carrell in hell. This makes sense in a public space where many people are having their first experience with handheld fire, but it is usually much more than is needed. Think of it this way: a jeweler needs to have control over a torch to a fraction of an inch. Move the torch a quarter-inch too close and a piece can be ruined. Given that level of precision, you really don't need to protect as if the torch is a flame thrower. I recommend a dedicated soldering area that is conveniently close to your jewelers bench and removed from direct light. I'm not concerned about a flame pointed sideways—I don't think you need to erect walls around the soldering area—but it is certain that the surface on which you work will take some abuse.

Soldering tables get wet with water, flux, and pickle. They can be scorched by an errant flame or when a piece rolls off the soldering block. I've never seen a soldering table catch fire, but I've never seen one I'd want to kiss either. Here are a couple suggestions for the soldering table:

- A discardable piece of plywood. Of course this will burn, but in practice, this is a matter of charred spots, not a raging fire. Splash a little water on the board at the end of a work day, and throw the board away when it gets nasty. I've seen people lay a sheet of metal over the plywood, but I don't recommend it. This is easier to clean up, but has the disadvantage of hiding a smoldering spot.

- Paving bricks. This is hard to beat for durability, and has long been a favorite with welders. The bricks will add at least two inches to the height of the table, which might be awkward in some cases, but if you are building a soldering stand you can compensate for this. Buy the bricks at a gardening, masonry, or lumber store, and lay them snugly side by side. It is not necessary to glue them down or to fill the spaces between the bricks with grout.

- Ceramic tiles. This is my favorite and I've used it for years. Buy any sort of tile and cement it onto a tabletop. I usually press the pieces close together, but you could use the standard spacing and add grout if you want to. I don't solder directly on this surface, but set a soft brick or soldering pad on it safely.

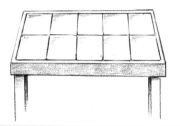

Ventilation

The need (or lack of need) for ventilation when soldering depends on the flux you are using, the kind of solder, the duration of your work and your own sensitivity to the fumes created. In the construction of a piece of jewelry, most of the time is usually devoted to shaping, filing, and sanding. Soldering events last a few minutes and might come only a few times a day. Compare that, for instance, to a soldering station in a factory where an employee might face a cart loaded with thousands of parts to be soldered together. Clearly the needs of one situation are different than the other. Factory owners: seek advice from experts in the field. The following information is not directed at you.

Very few metals emit dangerous fumes when they are melted, and even those don't typically pose a problem unless a large quantity of metal is superheated and poured, as in a foundry. Our goal in soldering—and you can write this down—is to not melt stuff.

The same applies to solder, though in this case, the alloy is intended to melt. Years ago, silver solder was made with a metal called cadmium, which greatly lowered the melting point. It was discovered that cadmium caused neurological and respiratory damage, so its use has been discontinued.

Of greater concern is flux, partly because there is more of it around during soldering, and partly because the vapors that are given off can be troublesome. The situation described above applies here. If you are a jeweler who spends 10–15 minutes of each work day with the torch in your hand, simple air exchange is usually sufficient. Insuring a movement of fresh air through the studio, can be as simple as opening a door on one side of the room and a window on the other. If a natural draft is not created, set a small fan in position to push fumes away from you. If you are a production worker who spends half your day at a soldering bench, you should consult ventilation experts and state health and safety specialists to devise an arrangement that will meet your needs.

Tweezers, Tongs, & Clips

I can't imagine a soldering station that isn't equipped with at least one (and usually two) of these tools. They can be purchased or made in the studio, expensive or basic, but sooner or later, you'll find yourself reaching for these. Soldering tweezers – 6" steel tweezers that are reserved for working directly in the flame. The tips will become corroded, which is why you'll want another pair that doesn't go in the flame.

Crosslock Tweezers – these tools open when pinched and stay closed when you set them down. This makes them handy to clutch pieces during soldering. One version has insulating plastic on the handles.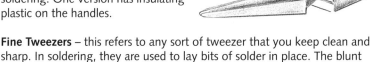

Fine Tweezers – this refers to any sort of tweezer that you keep clean and sharp. In soldering, they are used to lay bits of solder in place. The blunt tool you have in the medicine chest can work for this purpose, but it is a clumsy and inelegant tool compared to the standard 4" jeweler's tweezer. You can pay a lot for these, but for starters, a stainless steel tweezer that costs a few dollars is sufficient. The trick is to avoid using it in the flame.

Tongs – at the soldering station, this refers to copper, brass, or stainless steel tongs that are used to move a soldered piece into and out of the pickle bath. They can be made of two pieces like tweezers or from a single piece bent in a "U", as we see in ice tongs. Again, these can be purchased but are often made in the studio.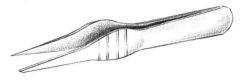

Clips – I'm referring here to a collection of gripping tools you make as you need them. The most common clip is a short piece of brass, nickel, or steel that has been bent into a "U" and hammered along its arc. The variations on this, in size, shape, and use, is tremendous. In addition to an assortment of these, I also keep a few large nuts and bolts on my soldering bench to help anchor pieces into place.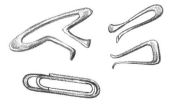

Spring Clips – Make these as needed from coat hanger wire, stainless welding rod, brass, or any other available rigid wire. These clamps are homemade versions of crosslock tweezers, and have the advantage of being shaped to meet specific needs and tensions. I have small ones I've made from paper clips and others large enough to hold handles onto large vessels.

Making a Spring Clip

Start by bending a loop in the center of a length of wire, ending so that the two arms are parallel and about the same length. An inch or two from the loop, bend each leg inward at a 45° angle. This will cause them to form an "X." Make another bend just past the crossing point to bring the two arms back to parallel. When you squeeze near the loop, the arms will open; at rest, the arms are pushing toward each other. To adjust the tension, pull the arms apart or press them together. Bend the tips into whatever shape will be useful.

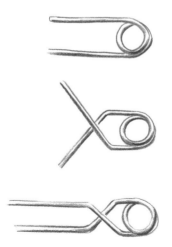

Useful Shapes

The value of making these clips yourself is that you can tailor them to specific needs. Clearly the possibilities are endless, and here are a few suggestions to get you started. The scale should also be modified to suit the situation—I find that large paperclips can be opened and rebent to make very handy clips.

Clips to hold halves of a bead together.

Clips to hold a setting onto a ring shank.

Soldering Investment

There are times when the pieces are too small, too numerous, or too oddly shaped to make clips practical. Wouldn't it be great if there was a moldable material that could hold the pieces in position while you soldered them? Well, there is—it's called soldering investment. Here's how to use it:

1 Prepare pieces as usual. As in any soldering operation, the pieces must be clean and they must fit together well.

2 Attach the pieces with epoxy or (faster), a cyanoacrylate like Super Glue.

3 Mix up a small quantity of soldering investment. This is a plaster-based material that has extra ingredients that allow it to withstand soldering temperatures. Conventional casting investment can be used, but it takes at least an hour to cure. Investment made for this purpose has been formulated to cure in a few minutes.

4 Add powder to water to make a thick creamy consistency, then daub this onto the work so that it surrounds all the parts and leaves the joint areas exposed. If investment flows onto the joint, wipe it away, and scrape off residue after it has hardened. Obviously, it's important that the joint itself is exposed and clean.

5 Apply flux and then a chip of solder onto each joint. Heat the entire assembly slowly to drive moisture out of the flux and cure the investment. When you are sure that no steam is rising, bring the torch closer and heat the parts until the solder flows.

6 Allow to sit for a few seconds to be sure the solder has set, then quench the piece in a dish of water. Most of the investment will crumble off; remove the rest with a toothbrush.

SUPPLIES
Solder
Traditional Silver Solder

In earlier times, it was normal for silversmiths and gold workers to refashion damaged or outdated goods into new objects. In the times before precise metallurgy and government regulations, it was common that a metalworker would not know the exact components of the alloy he was working with, nor was it likely that this alloy matched perfectly with other alloys in the shop. The idea of standard alloys and solders to match them are relatively recent developments.

In those earlier times, solder was made for each new batch of metal. When an ingot was poured, the smith cut off a small piece and further alloyed it to create a solder that would be appropriate for that particular mix. By adding a small amount of zinc, the silversmith was able to lower the melting point of the alloy while at the same time creating a metal with low viscosity (which meant it would penetrate nicely). We can imagine the smith cutting off a piece of this sample and setting it aside (marking it somehow), then remelting the remaining portion with a little more zinc to create a solder with an even lower melting point. The process could be repeated as often as necessary to fill the requirements of the project, though with each addition, the color shift became more obvious. For the record, it probably wasn't pure zinc that was added, because that metal has such a low melting point that some of the charge would vaporize before it could go into alloy. Instead, small pieces of brass were most often used. (Brass is an alloy of copper and zinc.)

In recent times, improved technology and the requirements of industry and trade have standardized the international precious metals industry. A century ago when the law read, in essence, "Sterling must be at least 92.5% silver," a refiner might choose to err on the side of caution so the alloy could be 93 or 93 1/2% silver. As measuring devices became more reliable, it was no longer necessary to add this little extra. Similarly, solders are consistently manufactured to exacting standards.

Contemporary Practice

In the jewelry world, three grades of solder are used for all silver work and for most work in copper and brass. These are sold by all refiners of precious metals and through any jewelry supply company. If there is a difference between these standard silver solders, it is so slight that only an expert or a well-equipped lab can detect it. After 30 years of soldering, I'd say that all easy solders act the same, as do all medium and hard solders.

Why Do I Need Three Solders?

The reason to have solders that melt at three distinct temperatures lies in the fact that the brazing action only works at high heat—and this much heat will spread throughout the piece. When assembling a piece with several joints, there is a risk that a first joint will come undone when you are working on a second joint. The solution to this is to systematically use grades of solder, starting with the highest melting first (illustration).

Forms of Solder

Just as brass, copper, or any other alloy can be purchased in several forms, silver solder is also sold as sheet and wire. The advantage of sheet is that you can cut exactly the size pieces you need, then position these small pieces (sometimes called *paillons*) just where you want the solder to be. The advantage of wire is that it can be fed into place during soldering, which eliminates the cutting and placing steps. Wire solder is also useful when a relatively large supply of solder is needed, for instance when filling an inlay.

All solder alloys look alike, so it's important to mark them well. Don't use markings that will fall off or fade, like masking tape, marker, or stickers. Instead, scratch or stamp a mark into sheet solder (E, M, and H come to mind), and make a unique (and rememberable) bend in solder wire.

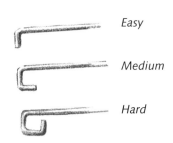

Easy

Medium

Hard

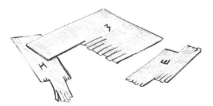

In sheet solder, stamp or scratch a code (like E, M, and H for instance). Don't use tape or stickers because they eventually dry out and fall off.

Gold Solder

Silver solders are relatively simple compared to gold solders, where there are more variables at work. All pure gold looks alike, but when copper, silver, or other metals are added to strengthen the alloy, subtle differences in proportion alter the color of the gold. Beyond the familiar yellow, white, green, and rose gold, there are designer shades. In addition, gold is commonly available in at least three grades of purity (10k, 14k, and 18k) with 20k and 22k gaining increased popularity.

The concept at work is the same as with silver: dilute the alloy slightly with a metal of lower nobility and the melting point goes down. This means that any lower karat alloy can be used as a solder for any higher karat alloy. A piece of 14k yellow gold can be used as a solder for 18k, for instance, but there will be a color disparity. Especially when you are working in gold with a lot of fabrication, it's a good idea to purchase solder at the same time as the metal, from the same refiner.

Gold Alloys and Their Melting Points

karat	gold	silver	copper	solidus range *			
22	91.6	4.2	4.2	1003 °C	971 °C	1837 °F	1780°F
20	83.3	8.3	8.3	955	915	1751	1680
18	75.0	12.5	12.5	905	882	1651	1620
16	66.6	16.7	16.7	872	855	1600	1571
14	58.5	20.75	20.75	845	827	1553	1521
12	50	25	25	827	807	1521	1485
9	37.5	31.25	31.25	825	790	1517	1454

Solidus Range: As an alloy cools from a liquid state, it starts to solidify at the first temperature shown, and becomes completely solid at the lower temperature.

From *Working in Precious Metals* by Ernest A. Smith. N.A.G. Press Limited, London, © 1950.

LOW-MELTING BRAZING ALLOYS

Silver brazing and variations on it are widely used in commercial and industrial situations, and for these, a wide range of alloys has been developed. Jewelers will find little need for these, but sculptors, modelmakers, and other people working with copper, brass, bronze, and steel might find them useful. These alloys often contain three, four, or more constituent metals and typically have a bronzy-brown color. They tend to be almost as strong as silver solder and often do not require flux. Unlike silver solders, these alloys can be mounded to fill a gap. Here are a couple popular members of this family, but there are others. Visit a local welding shop or metal fabrication company to learn more.

- Silvaloy A38T, Silvaloy A50N, Silvaloy A56T
- Dynaflow
- Stay-silv 15

Flux

Metals oxidize when exposed to air, creating a dark layer of scale. The formation is accelerated by heat, which means we find ourselves in a vicious cycle: we need heat to create spaces between crystals, we need an oxide-free surface for the solder to flow, and heat makes metal oxidize. The solution is to introduce a chemical that can reduce the formation of oxides, and we call this stuff *flux*.

Fluxes are chemical compounds designed to absorb oxides at specific temperatures. As described earlier, fluxes for soft solder are specific to those alloys and will be useless for silver brazing. The fluxes described below are made for high temperature brazing and can't be used for low temperature, lead-bearing solders. If in doubt, check the label of the flux container for the temperature range at which the flux is active.

For clarity we can divide brazing fluxes into two groups: borax-based and fluoride-based. Each has its benefits and shortcomings.

Borax-based fluxes
… are usually in the form of paste.
… develop a glassy layer that protects metal from oxides for
    long duration.
… are difficult to remove after soldering because the glassy
    layer bonds well to metal.
… can be dissolved in pickle or hot water.

Fluoride-based fluxes
... are usually a watery liquid, often yellow or green.
... do not develop a glassy skin. Because they do not require
pickle, they are sometimes called "self-pickling."
... are especially good for low-oxidation metals like gold.
... can be dissolved quickly in pickle or hot water.

Protective Flux

A secondary use of flux is to prevent the penetration of oxides into sterling and copper-bearing gold alloys, where they can create a permanent stain called firescale. Normal flux has this effect, but is generally limited to the area directly around the solder joint. Some metalsmiths choose to protect their work by applying a protective coating of flux over the entire piece before soldering.

Any paste flux can be used for this, but boric acid is the key ingredient for this purpose, and it can be used by itself. One solution is to mix boric acid into water and spritz this solution onto the metal. Because boric acid is not soluble in water, the white powder will quickly settle to the bottom, so you'll need to shake the bottle periodically as you apply it. A variation on this uses alcohol instead of water. Because the alcohol burns away quickly, this speeds up the coating process. Either dip the piece in a boric acid/alcohol mix or shake the mix and spritz it onto the work. Brush a flame across the piece and the alcohol will ignite. It quickly burns away and leaves a white crust of boric acid over the piece. While this is efficient, I do not recommend it because of the potential hazard of having a jar of flammable liquid near a soldering station. If you choose to use this, be careful to locate the jar where you cannot accidentally ignite the bottle.

Prip's Flux

This is a protective flux you make in the studio and apply by dipping or spritzing onto metal. The usual method is to warm the metal slightly, just to the point where it would be uncomfortable to hold in your hands. At that point, dip the piece in solution (if it's small) or spritz the solution onto the piece with a spray bottle. Either way, the goal is to create a crusty white coating. Repeat this step at least three times until you are sure the protective film has no gaps. An advantage of Prip's flux is that it is waterproof. If you are doing multiple solderings, quench only in water until after the last soldering operation. At that point, use pickle and the protective coating will dissovle.

Recipe for Prip's Flux

75 ml	BORAX
75 ml	TRISODIUM PHOSPHATE*
90 ml	BORIC ACID

*TSP is sold in hardware and paint stores for cleaning walls before painting. (Do not use a synthetic, non-phosphate version). Boil these ingredients in two quarts of water. They will not dissolve at room temperature, so the goal here is to force the chemicals into solution. This makes a concentrated solution that can be diluted with equal parts water to make it ready to use. If the solution crystalizes, warm it to redissolve the components.

PICKLE

Show me a soldering station without a pickle pot and I'll show you someone who's out refilling his pickle pot. Unless you're working with pure gold or platinum, all soldering operations will discolor metals. In all other cases, the oxide layer that is formed can be removed by mechanical abrasion (like sanding) but usually that's a bad idea. Once you've soldered parts together, it is wasteful and time-consuming, to rub the work with sandpaper. Goldsmiths a long time ago figured out that low-strength acidic solutions would remove the oxides without damaging the work. Because the earliest solution used for this was vinegar, which was also used to preserve vegetables, the cleansing bath came to be known as *pickle*. Even though we no longer use the same chemistry to flavor our cucumbers and clean our jewelry, the term has stuck.

Fact is, almost any acidic solution will have some value in removing oxides from metals. This would include sulfuric acid and other strong chemicals. We are fortunate in our time to have found other, less dangerous chemicals that do the job efficiently and safely. The most common in the jewelry community is sodium bisulfate ($NaHSO_4 \cdot H_2O$), sold commercially as a product called Sparex. Sodium bisulfate is a principle ingredient in the compound used to **lower** the pH in swimming pools. This might be helpful information if there are more pool and spa supply stores than jewelry companies in your area. Both of these versions will appear as a granular material that is dissolved in water to make a cleaning bath for metals. The solution works at room temperature but it works faster when warm. For this reason, many jewelers use a crock pot to keep the solution warm but not boiling. Any container used for this purpose should never again be used for foods.

Use bathtub caulking to seal all seams and joints.

There is a tendency to quench hot metal in pickle, but this is not recommended. There is a small risk of pickle being splashed into your face, but beyond that, this bad habit risks contaminating the metal by trapping chemicals inside the crystal structure. It is better to quench in water and then put the piece in pickle. This will add a minute or two to the time required to clean the metal, but insures stronger joints and a better finish.

Citric Acid as a Pickle

Jewelery supply companies sell a citric-based pickle, and in a pinch, you can use almost anything that contains citric acid. This includes lemon juice, orange soda, Fresca, and similar lemon or lime flavored drinks. Use at room temperature and allow several hours or overnight to remove oxides.

Hydrogen Peroxide

When brass is cleaned in Sparex, the metal will always be left with a pink-colored layer of copper. To remove this, make a special pickle solution using hydrogen peroxide (H_2O_2). This solution will lose its strength in an hour or two, so mix it up only when you are ready to use it. The "extra" oxygen molecule evaporates, leaving water (H_2O), which tells us that the pickle is still good to use, just that it has lost its brass-cleaning ability.

1 After all soldering is complete, clean the work in normal pickle to remove oxides.

2 Make up a fresh batch of Sparex using hydrogen peroxide instead of water. A typical concentration is a tablespoon of Sparex to a cup of peroxide, but this is not a critical measurement (i.e., you can eyeball it).

3 Warm the piece slightly and dip it into the solution. The rosy layer will dissolve in 10-20 minutes, leaving a bright yellow surface. If you leave work in this pickle for much longer than that, it can be etched and it can turn black. To remove the black layer, heat the work up and go through the above process again. The etching can't be reversed.

Nickel Pickle

This is a proprietary pickle whose active ingredients are sodium bisulfate and potassium dichromate. Sparex and similar pickles have little effect on nickel silver, and for many years the only alternative was to use nitric acid. Now we can use a proprietary solution that is sold through most large-scale jewelry suppliers, typically as granules that are dissolved in water.

Preparation for Soldering

Cleanliness

This is not simply a matter of looking clean, but of being chemically clean. A time-honored test for this is to sprinkle some water onto a piece of metal and watch the results. If the water draws up into beads, the metal is not clean. If metal fails this test, scrub it with soap and water or, even better, a mechanical scrub like steel wool, Scotch-Brite, or sandpaper. When the metal is clean, the water will spread in an even sheet over the surface, which is why this is called the "sheeting test."

Water droplets form on oily metal.

Water makes a smooth layer when the metal is clean.

Any cleaning is better than none, but some materials are better than others. Pumice is a traditional favorite because it is versatile, inexpensive, and chemically neutral. This is not true of soap, which has a very low pH, or steel wool, which is loaded with oil. Pumice is sold through hardware stores and jewelry suppliers as a coarse powder. It can be used dry or mixed with a little water to form a paste. A modern alternative that is similarly free of chemicals are the nylon scouring pads sold under the trade name of Scotch-Brite. Similar pads are also available through auto supply companies.

Fit

One of the phrases most often repeated in beginning metalsmithing classes is this: "Solder won't fill a gap." Soft solder makes a bridge across the space between parts, but silver solder achieves its strength by working at a much smaller level, penetrating the crystal structure of the metal itself. If the parts are not very close together, it is possible for the solder to penetrate two adjacent parts properly but fail to create a bond.

The standard test to insure that the parts are sufficiently aligned is to hold a piece up to a light. If the space between parts is larger than the thickness of a piece of paper, the gap is too large. Bend the parts or use a file or sawblade to make them fit better.

Use Flux

As described earlier, flux is needed to absorb oxygen that would otherwise combine with the metal to form a scale. Flux is usually applied with a brush, but in some situations it is more efficient to either spritz liquid flux or to dip small parts into flux. Use enough flux to be certain that it does not become oxygen-saturated before the solder flows, but not so much that a gooey coating makes it difficult to see the solder flow.

Heating

The goal is pretty easy to describe: bring all the parts being joined to the same temperature at the same moment. Easier said than done, especially if the pieces are of different size, thickness, and shape. Just as an experienced driver uses the gas, brakes, clutch, and the steering wheel in a fluid combination of actions to negotiate a curve, an experienced metalsmith is constantly making small and usually unconscious adjustments to the torch during soldering. The flame is sometimes turned up or down at the valve, the torch is tilted, lifted away from the metal, pushed closer for a few seconds, then tilted away slightly. These actions can't be described because they are different for each situation. Instead, a jeweler learns to read the temperature of metal by seeing its color, and from this, picks up subtle clues about what to do next.

Even Heating

As metal gets hotter, it goes through a sequence of color changes, and this is how we keep track of what's going on. Hold the torch so the flame is vertical or nearly vertical, and move it in a relaxed sweeping motion. When you first approach a prepared joint, keep the flame several inches above the metal to allow liquid in the flux to evaporate. Coming in too quickly causes the flux to boil, which can throw solder chips aside. It is more efficient to come in slowly than to rush things and spend time repositioning the solder.

When the flux becomes crusty and shows no further boiling movement, lower the torch until the tip of the inner cone is about three-quarters of an inch from the metal. Think of a 4" target with the solder joint in the middle, and start by moving the torch around the largest circle. Observe the color changes in the various units and direct the torch so that all the parts go through the same colors simultaneously. When one piece turns pale gray, see that the other parts also turn pale gray. When one part starts to show a dull red, move the torch onto other parts so they reach the same color. Continue in this way until all the parts reach the soldering temperature. Colors are easiest to see in a dimly lit area.

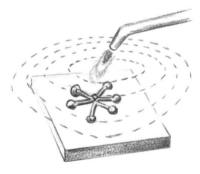

And how will you know when you have reached that temperature? It's impossible to describe on paper, but relatively easy to learn. All you need to do is make a thousand solder joints and you'll know—nothing to it! How do you know when to shift from third gear to fourth, or when to flip a fried egg? The answers have to do with vision, smell, hearing, intuition, and experience. The same is true for soldering. There is simply no substitute for experience.

Other Factors in Heating: Heat Sinks

A heat sink is any material or object that draws heat away from where you want it. In most cases this is something to avoid, but there are times when creative metalsmiths will use heat sinks to help during soldering. Imagine a very small piece that is being attached to a much larger one. Clearly the large piece needs to get most of the heat, but perhaps doing this risks melting the small piece. By gripping it in tweezers (which take up some of the heat), the smaller unit is somewhat protected.

Another example: If you are soldering onto a piece that has a heat-sensitive section, make a barrier with a heat sink (like the large bolt shown here). This stops the flow of heat through the piece.

One more: Water is a great heat sink, and has the advantage of shaping itself neatly around an area you want to protect. Here is a traditional method for protecting a ring with a stone.

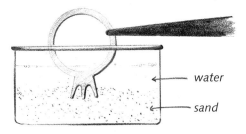

water

sand

Clean Up After Soldering

As mentioned above, it is not good practice to quench hot metal in pickle. Instead, allow the metal to cool until the red has completely disappeared before quenching in water. Only then should the work be transferred to pickle. Retrieve the piece with copper, brass, or stainless tongs, and rinse it well in water. If this rinse is midway in the fabrication process, a simple dip in a pan of water is sufficient, but after the final dip in pickle, use a more aggressive method to be sure that no pickle remains in recesses.

In many cases it is sufficient to hold the work under running water. Rotate the work so all surfaces are flushed clean. If there are crevices, crannies, or interior spaces, even this might not be enough. Pickle left on a piece will eventually make itself known, usually as a crusty acidic growth that will ruin patinas (and sometimes a wearer's clothing). To avoid this problem, mix a strong solution of baking soda and water. You don't need to get out measuring spoons—put a handful of soda into a couple cups of water and stir well. Immerse the work and stir it so the neutralizing solution has a chance to reach into tight spots. Some people like to boil this solution. The heat doesn't increase the chemical action, but the boiling agitates the work so the solution reaches everywhere. In extreme cases, like beads with small holes, it might be necessary to use a syringe to forcibly inject the baking soda solution into the interior. Another alternative is to use the microscopic action of an ultrasonic machine for this purpose. Rather than replace the soapy solution with a neutralizing baking soda bath, float a small dish in the ultrasonic and fill that dish with the baking soda solution.

Removing Excess Solder

The best way to remove excess solder is to avoid it in the first place. I speak from experience when I say that it is tempting to use solder pieces that are close at hand, even when you know they are too large, rather than interrupt the process to cut fresh solder. It's tempting to continue, but don't. The time it takes to control the amount of solder you use is a fraction of the time needed to remove the blob of solder that results from having too much. More than time, the process of removing solder can erode a surface and undermine the crisp confidence of your work. Even when you use a small amount of solder, it still happens that the solder can flow onto surfaces where it must be removed. Each situation is unique and each person has his or her own preferred methods, but here are a few approaches that are worth a try:

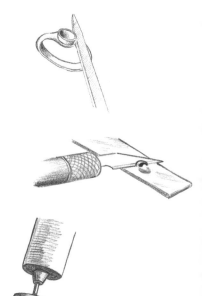

- Scrape or carve excess solder with a knife. As simple as this seems, most people forget that metal can be whittled away like wood. Use a razor knife, scalpel, or similar sharp tool to gently shave curls of solder off. It's better to take several shallow cuts than one deep one.

- Use a delicate file to reach into tight spots. To have full control, it is important to limit the active edges of the file. If your small files have teeth on all sides, use a grinding wheel to smooth one side as needed.

- Pumice wheel. This is a rubber wheel embedded with a fine natural abrasive. Pumice wheels are to jewelry what pink erasers are to high school... really handy.

- Gravers are hardened steel tools used to cut metal. We usually think of them as something to cut initials and romantic sentiments into ring shanks, but they can also be used to slice away extra bits of solder. Use a flat graver or the side of a square graver. As mentioned above, it's better to make several shallow strokes than a few aggressive digs.

Not Recommended

When there is excess solder, the best advice is to remove it as cleanly and completely as possible. The techniques above will accomplish this. Here are a few techniques that are not recommended, either because they do not remove material, or because they do not offer pinpoint accuracy.

- **Burnishing**
  Bad idea. This technique moves existing metal around, but does not remove it. Not only will it not solve the problem, but it will often make the problem more obvious.

- **Tumbling**
  This is a mechanical version of burnishing, and it has the same drawbacks, only worse. Tumbling makes existing surfaces shiny, but it does not significantly alter the shape of those surfaces. In other words, tumbling will leave your solder blobs shiny, but it won't remove them.

- **Sanding**
  Sandpaper can sometimes be used to remove solder, but because solder is often harder than the metals being joined, it has a tendency to wear down the adjacent metal more than it reduces the excess solder. If you use papers, be aggressive (i.e., use a large grit), and wrap the paper around a stiff tool like a ruler to gain better leverage.

WELDING
Definition & Overview

Welding is a process of joining parts by making the surface of all components fluid or plastic. Sometimes with the addition of force, and sometimes with the introduction of additional material, the substance of the parts flows together to become a single unit. Welds are as strong as their parent metal because they *are* the parent metal.

We most often think of welding as particular to steel, but many widely diverse materials lend themselves to welding, including pewter, platinum, and plastic. I'll touch on these, but let's start with steel.

Forge Welding

It is probably a safe guess that forge welding dates back to the same time as the development of refining methods to convert iron ore to steel. We know that early ingots were coarse, and that impurities were driven out by hammering the steel at red heat. It would be only a matter of time before an enterprising blacksmith tried working on two pieces at once. He would have discovered that if he set two very hot pieces of steel together and struck them, the molten materials at the surface flowed together and hardened into a single block.

He would have also discovered that the presence of impurities in the area weakened the bond, and that a layer of sand helped to float these impurities away. And here we are, at least three millenia later, and forge welding is still done the same way.

1 Prepare the pieces to be joined so they fit well together.

2 Scrape, grind, or file off surface oxides (rust).

3 Heat the steel to a glowing, liquid-looking white heat, applying borax powder once or twice as the heat develops. Both pieces must reach this temperature at the same time.

4 Quickly set the parts together and strike a series of rapid blows to force the molten parts to join.

5 Allow to cool down to a dull red color, then quench in water.

Equipment

In theory, any device that will bring the steel to the necessary temperatures (around 2730° F, 1500° C) can be used for forge welding. In practice, the most common tool is a coal-fired hearth or forge. This time-honored tool uses a blower to force air into a coal fire to develop a lasting, even, and affordable heat. Pieces of steel are laid into the fire until they reach welding temperature. At that point they are grasped in sturdy steel tongs and laid across a heavy steel anvil where they are struck with a large hammer, usually with a crowned face. Other tools needed are a leather apron (this process throws a lot of sparks), goggles, and hearing protection.

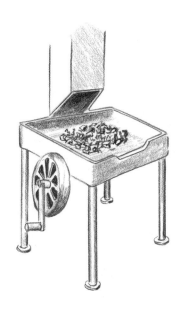

Supplies

Besides the coal to fuel the fire, forge welding requires only a flux. Commercial fluxes are sold by welding and blacksmithing supply companies, and many smiths make their own from borax. Borax in its common form is anhydrous, which means it has a tendency to pick up moisture from the air. Even though the powder appears to be dry, when it is sprinkled onto hot metal, the moisture comes out as steam, blowing the lightweight powder off the metal. To prevent this, heat the borax powder in a ceramic or steel vessel until it melts into a gooey syrup. When it cools, this will harden into glass. Break this into pieces, then grind it in a mortar and pestle to create a fine white powder. Though this looks almost identical to the original borax, this version will not puff away when it hits the hot metal.

Eye Protection

The intense flame of a welding torch emits rays that will damage eyesight, so it is important to always wear protective covering. These are not just very dark sunglasses, but industrial strength darkened glass specifically designed to shield against specific ultraviolet and infrared light waves emitted during welding.

Lenses

Because welding lenses are so dark, it is difficult, sometimes impossible, to see through them under normal lighting conditions. For this reason, traditional goggles and masks have flip up lenses. A recent development uses an electronic device (either battery or solar powered) to instantly darken a clear lens when a spark is struck. These are expensive, but offer the best option in both protection and versatility.

Lenses are identified by their relative darkness in a scale of shades that runs from 1 to 14, sometimes written as UVIR #5, for instance, in reference to the ultraviolet and infrared waves that are being filtered out. The chart here shows that as the power of your welding apparatus goes up, so does the danger of eye damage, and so should your level of protection. It is always better to be on the high side of these recommendations rather than on the low.

Lens Numbers and Recommended Applications

Shade 5   Light gas welding

6 & 7   Light gas welding and arc welding up to 30 amps

8 & 9   Heavy gas welding and arc welding up to 75 amps

10 & 11   Arc welding and cutting in the range of 75–200 amps

12   Arc welding and cutting in the range of 200–400 amps

13 & 14   Arc welding and cutting over 400 amps

Helmets

Welding helmets are available in a wide range of sizes, shapes, and cost. Most are made of a dense plastic and have an interior web (like a bike helmet) to lift the helmet off your head. Only one thing can be said about all of them—they make a great impression when you wear one to a party. Beyond that, selection will depend on your personal needs, your budget, and the intensity of the torch you are using. The lenses in most helmets (and some goggles) are covered by an inexpensive clear glass lens. This will become pitted as it is struck by sparks, and should be replaced as soon as visibility is compromised.

Goggles

Goggles are small, relatively lightweight eye protection that cover only the eyes. Most welding eyewear will fit snugly against the face to protect against sparks and bits of debris that might otherwise enter from the side. Goggles are the cheapest form of eye protection, but they are not ideal because they can become uncomfortable after a few hours of wear.

Gloves and Aprons

Welding makes sparks, period. Unless you like wearing lace and looking like a cheetah, see that you are properly covered with clothing that will protect you from small particles of hot metal. Traditionally this has meant leather aprons and jackets, and those are still in wide use. They are heavy and can be a bit awkward, but they do the job.

It should be obvious that this applies to hand protection too, especially because your hands are very close to the welding area. Strong leather gloves that will not allow stray sparks to enter at the wrist are mandatory. Welders will quickly develop a nose for burning leather (not a pleasant smell) because it tells them their glove is doing its job, and that a hot piece of metal is close at hand.

Holding Jigs

Most welding operations, especially gas welding, require the welder to use both hands to complete the weld—one holding the torch and the other to feed welding rod into the puddle of molten metal that is created. This means you will not be able to hold pieces in place during welding. For this reason, clamps are an important part of a welder's toolbox.

Perhaps the most widely used tool for this are Vise-grip pliers. These locking pliers come in many sizes and configurations and can be modified (by welding, of course) to meet specific needs. Other holding tools include adjustable stands, vises, and C-clamps.

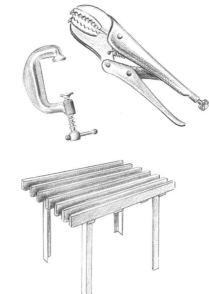

While it is not technically a holding jig, a welding table should be mentioned here. This is typically a sturdy table made of steel, roughly two by three feet, and standing at a convenient height for the welder. Instead of a solid top, a welding table is made of steel bars on edge. This open surface provides plenty of support, and creates many opportunities for clamping, while it provides a surface that is not as much of a heat sink as it would if it were solid. It also resists warping, which would almost certainly happen if welding was attempted on a flat steel surface.

Types of Welds

Most joints fall into one of these categories.

- **Butt weld**
  This describes two pieces of the same or similar thickness, meeting edge to edge.

- **Lap joint**
  This joint is the result of parts overlapping one another. Typically you weld the exposed edge on both sides.

- **Edge joint**
  This joint comes when the edge of one piece sits on the surface of another piece.

MODERN WELDING

Of course forge welding works as well now as it ever did, and a recurrence of interest in blacksmithing in the US since the 1970s insures that there are still artists among us who maintain this tradition. Their number is dwarfed, however, by the thousands of professional welders who go to work each day to assemble our washing machines, lawnmowers, cookware, and architecture. And that doesn't count the battalions of robots who are putting our cars together. Welding in the 20th century falls into three primary groups—gas, electric, and laser welding. Each of these deserves a book to itself, and in fact, each has dozens of books dedicated to its intricacies. The goal here is to provide a broad overview that will prepare you for further research into the method that best answers your needs.

Gas Welding

History

There was a time when most farms and ranches had a coal forge and an anvil—and someone who knew how to use them. This speaks to the importance of welding, and explains why advancements in welding technology have been eagerly accepted over the years. As the world became more mobile, the bulk and awkwardness of a coal forge became more troublesome. In the late 1800s, it became possible to fill steel bottles with acetylene and liquified oxygen. These fuels created temperatures high enough to melt steel, opening the door to the welding technology that dominated the 20th century.

Advantages

- Heat is brought to the joint rather than the other way around. This makes gas welding easier when dealing with large or heavy pieces.
- The equipment is relatively compact.
- Because it is not necessary to build a coal fire, the process is much faster.
- Though advanced welding is complex, the basics of the process are relatively easy to learn (compared with the full knowledge of blacksmithing needed for forge welding).

Equipment
Torches

By far the most common gas welding system uses acetylene and oxygen, gases that are liquified and trapped into steel cylinders. In most cases, these tanks are leased from a local supplier, a company that bears the responsibility of insuring that they are in good repair. Tanks are available in several sizes (measured in cubic feet of gas) to suit various needs.

The gas is under pressure, which means it will come out fast at first and slower as the pressure inside the tank decreases. To even out this force, all tanks must be fitted with a regulator, a compact valve that contains the pressure and allows the gas to exit at a controlled rate. Full safety information about regulators is available from suppliers of welding equipment and from many sources online, but a few basics warrant mention here.

– Match the regulator to the gas. They are specific.

– Never force a regulator onto a threaded joint. If threads are damaged, don't force it.

– Always check fittings after hooking up a fresh tank. Brush or spray soapy water onto all threaded connections to test for bubbles. If you see bubbles, tighten further. If the bubbles persist, swap the tank for a new one (or have the regulator repaired).

– Never use tape or other aids to make a tight joint.

– Always see that the regulator is in the "off" or open position before opening the tank valve.

Electric (Arc) Welding
History

Arc welding was discovered in suburban DesMoines in 1969 when little Johnny Smith reached into the toaster with a butterknife. OK, that's not true. In fact, it was patented in Britain in 1885, and in the US two years later, by two men named Benardos and Olszewski. In arc welding, a current of electricity is run through a conductive rod and the piece of metal that is being welded. When the circuit is opened up a short distance, a jolt of electricity jumps across the gap, creating a high temperature arc.

In practice, a welding machine is plugged into an electrical source (like a wall outlet or a generator), and two wires are extended from it. One is connected to the workpiece and the other has a rod contained in an insulated handle. The welder controls the flow and strength of the current. When the circuit is closed—that is, when the tip of the rod is touched to the connected piece of metal—a loud crackling spark is created. A welder holds the tip of the rod above the metal just enough to maintain the arc. Too much gap and the arc disappears; too close and the rod becomes welded to the workpiece. The rod can be used only to create the electric arc, or, more commonly, it can achieve this and simultaneously provide filler metal to reinforce the seam.

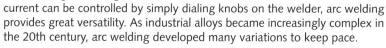

Electric welding is cleaner and faster than gas welding. Because the current can be controlled by simply dialing knobs on the welder, arc welding provides great versatility. As industrial alloys became increasingly complex in the 20th century, arc welding developed many variations to keep pace.

Spot Welding (Resistance Welding)
This variation also uses a jolt of electricity, but in this case is passed through the metals being joined rather than across a gap. This kind of welding cannot join a seam, but is widely used to join parts in everything from utensils to toys to cars. As mentioned earlier, a small scale version of this technique specifically designed for jewelry applications is called the Sparkie.

Shielded Metal Arc Welding (SMAW)
It is inevitable that oxygen and other atmospheric gasses will enter the pool of molten metal during welding, and in most cases these will compromise the strength or appearance of the weld. An ingenious way to minimize the effect of these gasses is to sheild the molten metal with an inert gas that prevents them from reaching the hot zone. To do this, a bottle of an inert gas like argon or nitrogen is attached to a hose that runs along the welding handle. Gas is fed through this tube during welding so it covers the weld. Besides making the weld stronger, this step usually also makes the joint neater, which shortens clean up time.

Welding Rods

In gas welding, the rods used to supply extra metal into the weld puddle are usually nothing more than convenient sized round wires of mild steel. Rods for arc welding (which are called electrodes), not only carry current to the weld, but supply additional material and often flux. Rods are available in sizes from 1/16" to 5/16" and in a variety of alloys. They are often coated with a crusty layer of flux that melts as the rod comes into the arc to create a liquid that removes oxides and slag from the weld.

Rods are identified by a numeric code called A.W. S. after the American Welding Society that created the system. The code tells whether the rod can be used for alternating current (AC), direct current (DC), or both types of welding. It will also describe the tensile strength of the finished weld, and what orientations are most appropriate for that particular rod.

Matching Current to Rod

The larger the workpiece, the more current is needed to get it to welding temperature. And the higher the amperage, the larger the rod needed to carry it effectively. Here are some general guidelines, though any given application might require some fine tuning.

Recommended Rod, Amp, and Thickness Schedules

Electrode Diameter	Amp Range	Plate (the work)
1/16"	20–40	Up to 3/16"
3/32"	40–125	Up to 1/4"
1/8"	75–185	Over 1/8"
5/32"	105–250	Over 1/4"
3/16"	140–305	Over 3/8"
1/4"	210–430	Over 3/8"
5/16"	275–450	Over 1/2"

Part Three

Adhesives

HISTORY OF ADHESIVES

We tend to think of adhesives as relatively modern, but they go back a long way. The pharaohs of ancient Egypt slept on bed whose wooden frames were assembled with glue. And remarkably, they are still together, all these centuries later.

Early glues were made from animal or vegetable materials. Wax, gathered from bees or made from plants, was probably used first to attach feathers to arrow shafts. Archeologists have also found tree resins and tar used to join and waterproof crockery and boats. It was found that proteins have the ability to dry or cure into rigid, bonding substances. Common sources for protein include blood, egg white, and animal parts like bones, hooves, and horns. These were typically boiled, extracted, and mixed with a binder like clay or ground shells to create workable glue.

These materials are still used today, though they are quickly losing ground to synthetics. Most adults will remember that the icon for Elmer's Glue is a cow named Elsie. This was not a random selection, since the white glue of our childhoods was made from casein, a milk-based protein. Another familiar reference to natural glues is mucilage, the gooey glue in familiar bottles with a rubber tip. This glue, mostly associated with fixing paper to paper, is made from secretions of plants. Leather workers will be familiar with hide glue, also known as rabbit skin glue. It comes from animals… we'll leave it at that. In the mid-eighteenth century, a patent for an adhesive based on fish protein was filed in Great Britain.

In modern times, huge developments have been made in the discovery and refinement of synthetic glues. These are generally categorized as drying glues, hot glues, and reactive adhesives. Details of each can be found on the following pages.

It is difficult to overestimate the importance of glues in our lives. While we might not think of them as central to our work in a jewelry studio, consider the importance of adhesives in making sandpapers, polishing compounds, and tools.

NATURAL GLUES

Hide Glue

These adhesives are made from collagen derived from animal sources, typically rendered from the skins, hooves, or bones of animals. The glue is sold as a light-colored powder that is mixed with water to prepare for use. The typical mix is 50/50, though experimentation is required. One of the advantages of hide glue is that it can be modified to match specific needs. Adding more or less water is one way to accomplish this, and another is by adjusting the temperature of the glue for application.

Hide glue does not cure through evaporation, but sets up as the glue cools from its honey-like consistency to room temperature. Because individual products will vary, follow manufacturer's directions carefully. Here is a general idea of how to use hide glue.

1 Mix the powder with clean warm water. Stirring well. Allow to sit for several hours or overnight.

2 Warm the glue in a double boiler or on a low-temperature heat source like a coffee mug warmer. The glue must reach a certain temperature to become fluid, but overheating can ruin the glue, so it is important to be cautious.

3 The surfaces to be joined should be at normal room temperature. If they are not, use local heat like a lightbulb or hairdryer to warm them up.

4 Bring the glue to a gooey, drip-able viscosity and apply it to both surfaces to be joined. Hold or clamp until the glue sets, which can be only a matter of a few minutes. Allow to cure completely, which might take several hours.

5 One of the advantages of hide glue is that joints can be made to loosen by reapplying heat. This means that parts can come apart with little or no damage to the components.

Casein Glue

Casein is a protein found in fresh milk. It is extracted by mixing with chemicals, like acids or rennet, and has been used for centuries, going at least as far back as the ancient Egyptians. Casein glue has only moderate strength, but is sufficient for household uses. Casein is an important ingredient in casein paint, also known as milk paint.

DRYING GLUES

Polymers

Polymers are long molecular chains made up of similar or almost similar units. These commonly involve carbon, but can also be based on oxygen as the fundamental structural unit. Polymers include organic materials such as proteins and inorganics, an example of which are the long fibers used in Kevlar.

$$\leftarrow \overset{\displaystyle H}{\underset{\displaystyle H}{C}} - \overset{\displaystyle H}{\underset{\displaystyle H}{C}} - \overset{\displaystyle H}{\underset{\displaystyle H}{C}} - \overset{\displaystyle H}{\underset{\displaystyle H}{C}} - \overset{\displaystyle H}{\underset{\displaystyle H}{C}} \rightarrow$$

In a process called polylmerization, basic, usually simple monomers, are linked together, a bit like assembling beads into a necklace. Synthetic polymers account for many of our glues today, but the chemical mechanism is the same in the natural glues described on the previous page.

Polyvinyl Acetate

These adhesives are probably what most of us think about when we think "glue." Familiar Elmer's falls into this category, as does SOBO, TiteBond, and Duco Cement. As we know from grade school experience, these glues harden by evaporation. As a solvent (water, alcohol, or something else) goes off into the air, what remains cures into an adhesive. Changes in the formulations allow these glues to be waterproof, transparent, flexible, etc.

Hot Melt Glues

Many people are familiar with glue guns in which a finger-sized rod of plastic is pressed through a heated nozzle. The glue is a thermoplastic that becomes fluid at a relatively low temperature and then hardens when it cools to room temperature. These adhesives are not especially strong, but for simple everyday joining tasks, they can be very handy.

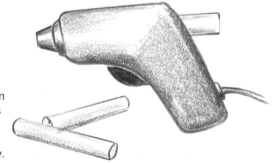

THERMOSETTING ADHESIVES

Epoxy

These now-familar two-part adhesives are created by combining a polymer with a catalyzing agent called a hardener. The first viable epoxies were developed in the mid-1930s, and today epoxies are used in industry, painted coatings, and yes, even to attach stones to jewelry.

Which One to Use

A well stocked hardware store will offer several choices of epoxy, and this is only a small sample of the scores of varieties that exist. In general the differences focus on color, length of cure time, and working time. While the strength of the resulting bond is slightly different for the various types, this is not usually relevant for studio applications. The fact is, epoxies are really strong, period. To say it another way, the weakest epoxy is still much stronger than the strongest non-epoxy. A possible exception is hide glue, which is amazingly tenacious when properly prepared.

Preparation Matters

There is a reason why we don't give epoxy to children—it is not an open-and-squirt adhesive. Careful preparation and mixing is important to get the full adhesive value from any two-part adhesive.

1 Design the work to provide as much surface contact as possible.

2 The surface should be broad, clean, and dry. Use sandpaper, pumice, or a file to create a roughened surface that is free of oil and dirt.

3 Epoxies cure through a chemical reaction called polymerization, and this requires that molecules of resin are brought into contact with molecules of hardener. To accomplish this, it is necessary to stir the mixture very well (or to knead well in the case of epoxy putty).

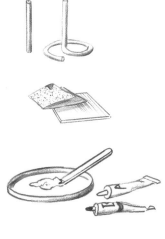

4 Allow the epoxy to cure without being jiggled. Clamping is not usually necessary for epoxy because it will fill a gap, but clamps are sometimes helpful to keep parts from moving.

SPECIALTY ADHESIVES

Cyanoacrylates – $C_5H_5NO_2$

If you are old enough to remember black and white TV, you can also remember the revolutionary Superglue, and the wacky commercials that showed its fantastic properties. The clear, acrylic resin was developed in the 1950s, originally when seeking a clear adhesive for aircraft canopies. Today there are several varieties on the market, all with similar strength and working properties.

The polymerization of cyanoacrylates is triggered by trace amounts of water, specifically, the hydroxide ions. Since water is almost always in the air in at least minute amounts, this explains why CA (as cyanoacrylate is known industrially) will bond almost anything.

As most of us know firsthand, one substance that contains trace amounts of moisture is skin, which is why, when you touch a drop on a tabletop to wipe it away, you immediately end up wearing a table. These glues are less appropriate for porous surfaces (e.g., attaching paper to wood) because they can be extremely dry. In such cases, lightly dampen one part and apply the glue to the other.

Original cyanocrylates were water-clear liquids, but over the years, manufacturers have created CAs in a range of consistencies, from paste to gel. The more viscous glues are better when you don't want the glue to run into adjacent areas and when working other than flat.

To remove CA (i.e., to get your hand off the table), use a small amount of acetone on a cloth or cotton swab. Acetone is an ingredient in many brands of nail polish remover. Note that acetone is a strong solvent and might damage or discolor some materials.

Ultra Violet Curing Adhesives

These adhesives are polymerized in the presence of ultraviolet light. While it is possible to achieve the reaction in prolonged sunlight, it is far more common to trigger the hardening reaction with a special lamp. In most cases, a nearly invisible yet very strong bond can be made in 3–5 minutes.

UV adhesives are used to join metal, glass, and plastic, in any arrangement that will allow light to penetrate. There are a wide variety of UV adhesives on the market, some with minor differences, but in most cases, a familiar "black light" sold at hardware and pet stores (for aquariums) is all that is needed. Read label directions for specific requirements.

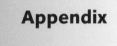

Appendix

Equivalent Numbers

B&S	mm	inches	drill #
0	8.5	.325	21/64
1	7.34	.289	9/32
2	6.52	.257	1/4
3	5.81	.229	7/32 · 1
4	5.18	.204	13/64 · 6
5	4.62	.182	3/16 · 15
6	4.11	.162	5/32 · 20
7	3.66	.144	9/64 · 27
8	3.25	.128	1/8 · 30
9	2.90	.114	33
10	2.59	.102	38
11	2.31	.091	3/32 · 43
12	2.06	.081	5/64 · 46
13	1.83	.072	50
14	1.63	.064	1/16 · 51
15	1.45	.057	52
16	1.30	.051	54
17	1.14	.045	3/64 · 55
18	1.02	.040	56
19	0.914	.036	60
20	0.812	.032	1/32 · 65
21	0.711	.028	67
22	0.635	.025	70
23	0.558	.022	71
24	0.508	.020	74
25	0.457	.018	75
26	0.406	.016	1/64 · 77
27	0.355	.014	78
28	0.304	.012	79
29	0.279	.011	80
30	0.254	.010	

Melting Points

	°F	°C
Tin	450	232
Lead	621	327
Aluminum	1220	660
Yellow Brass	1749	954
NuGold	1886	1030
Bronze	1945	1060
Copper	1981	1083
Nickel silver	2030	1110
Steel	2750	1511
Titanium	3272	1800
14K yellow gold	1476	802
18K yellow gold	1620	882
Sterling silver	1640	920
Fine silver	1762	961
Fine gold	1945	1063
Platinum	3225	1774

Temperature Conversions

Celsius to Fahrenheit

- Multiply the degrees C times 9
- Divide this number by 5
- Add 32

Fahrenheit to Celsius

- Subtract 32 from the degrees F
- Multiply this number by 5
- Divide by 9

°C	°F	°C	°F		°F	°C	°F	°C
0	32	650	1202		32	0	1300	704
50	122	675	1247		100	38	1350	732
75	167	700	1382		150	66	1400	760
100	212	725	1337		200	93	1450	788
125	257	750	1382		250	121	1500	816
150	302	775	1427		300	149	1550	843
175	347	800	1470		350	177	1600	871
200	392	825	1517		400	204	1650	871
225	437	850	1562		450	232	1700	927
250	482	875	1607		500	260	1750	954
275	527	900	1652		550	288	1800	982
300	572	925	1697		600	316	1850	1010
325	617	950	1742		650	343	1900	1038
350	662	975	1787		700	371	1950	1066
375	707	1000	1832		750	399	2000	1093
400	752	1025	1877		800	427	2050	1121
425	797	1050	1922		850	454	2100	1149
450	842	1075	1967		900	482	2150	1177
475	887	1100	2012		950	510	2200	1204
500	932	1125	2057		1000	538	2250	1232
525	977	1150	2102		1050	566	2300	1260
550	932	1175	2147		1100	593	2350	1288
575	1067	1200	2192		1150	621	2400	1316
600	1112	1225	2237		1200	649	2450	1343
625	1157	1250	2282		1250	677	2500	1371

Argentice 0870/286-3557
34 Harlech Crescent
Sketty, Swansea SA2 9LN
www.argentice.co.uk

Europ Findings
5-9 Hatton Wall
London, EC1N 8HX
www.eurunts.co.uk

Ballou Findings 01908 569 311
15 Cochran Close
Crownhill, Milton Keynes MK8 0AJ
www.ballou.com

Exchange Findings 0207/831-7574
49 Hatton Garden 0207/430-2028 fax
London, EC1N 8YS
www.cooksgold.com/trade-hatton.htm

Bellore Ltd. 0207/404-3220
39 Greville Street
London, EC1N 8PJ

Kernowcraft Rocks and Gems
Bollingey 01872/573-888
Perranporth 01872/573-704 fax
Cornwall, TR6 0DH
www.kernowcraft.co.uk
info@kernowcraft.com

J. Blundell & Son
16 Hatton Wall
London, EC1N 8JH

Rainbow Silks 01494/862-111
85 High Street 01494/862-651 fax
Great Missenden
Bucks, HP16 0AL
www.rainbowsilks.co.uk
caroline@rainbowsilks.co.uk

Capital Gems 0207/253-3575
30B Great Sutton Street 0207/251-9368 fax
Clerkenwell,
London EC1V 0DU
www.capitalgems.com
info@capitalgems.com

Rashbel Marketing 0207/831-5646
24-28 Hatton Wall
London, EC1N 8JH
www.rashbel.com
order@rashbel.com

Cookson Precious Metals
43 Hatton Garden 0207/400-6500
London, EC1N 8EE
www.cooksongold.com

Sutton Tools 0121/236-7139
Thomas Sutton (B'ham) Ltd.
37-38 Frederick Street
Birmingham, B1 3HN
www.suttontools.co.uk

craftsgemz.co.uk 01422/244-389
PO Box 711
Halifax, HX2 8WU
West Yorkshire
www.craftgemz.co.uk
info@craftgemz.co.uk

H.S. Walsh & Sons Ltd. 0207/242-3711
44 Hatton Garden
London, EC1N 8ER